DECODING
THE MYSTERY
of
WHEN WILL JESUS
RETURN

*"But you, brethren, are not in darkness,
so that this Day should surprise you as a thief"
(1 Thessalonians 5:4, NIV).*

RAYMOND J. MOORE

WESTBOW
PRESS®
A DIVISION OF THOMAS NELSON
& ZONDERVAN

This book is a work of non-fiction. Unless otherwise noted, the author and the publisher make no explicit guarantees as to the accuracy of the information contained in this book and in some cases, names of people and places have been altered to protect their privacy.

WestBow Press books may be ordered through booksellers or by contacting:

WestBow Press
A Division of Thomas Nelson & Zondervan
1663 Liberty Drive
Bloomington, IN 47403
www.westbowpress.com
1 (866) 928-1240

Because of the dynamic nature of the Internet, any web addresses or links contained in this book may have changed since publication and may no longer be valid. The views expressed in this work are solely those of the author and do not necessarily reflect the views of the publisher, and the publisher hereby disclaims any responsibility for them.

Any people depicted in stock imagery provided by Thinkstock are models, and such images are being used for illustrative purposes only. Certain stock imagery © Thinkstock.

ISBN: 978-1-9736-0305-4 (sc)
ISBN: 978-1-9736-0306-1 (hc)
ISBN: 978-1-9736-0304-7 (e)

Library of Congress Control Number: 2017914516

Print information available on the last page.

WestBow Press rev. date: 10/02/2017

CONTENTS

ACKNOWLEDGMENTS

I would like to recognize the many scholars and students of end-time prophecy, who give themselves toward the study and proclamation of this unique Christian doctrine. Teachers like Dr. Norman Holmes (my former Bible college professor), Dr. Jack Van Impe, Perry Stone, Randall Price, and Joel Rosenberg are among the many experts who have inspired me and gave me a strong desire in the study of end-time prophecy.

Together we continue to study and teach eschatology within the framework of scriptural context. Let us do so with grace, while being humble and open to the Holy Spirit and others for further and deeper revelation(s). Together we are bringing to the forefront this important doctrine (eschatology) to highlight the times in which we live and to awaken the Church of Jesus Christ to greater purpose and urgency in the midst of a world that seeks to deceive us.

INTRODUCTION

"But Jesus said, '... of that day and hour no one knows, not even the angels of heaven, but My Father only'" (Matt. 24:36). This scripture may easily be the first of many that may naturally come to one's mind in challenging what this book sets out to reveal. However, the timing of the return of Jesus Christ is not as blurred as the commonly accepted teachings within the Church may suggest. Thus, this book will challenge the normal thinking regarding Jesus' return and the various events surrounding this time frame.

When the apostle Paul was referring to the return of Jesus for the rapture of the Church, he made an interesting declaration that is often overlooked or misunderstood. He said, "Behold I tell you a *mystery*" (1 Cor. 15:51, 52). What the apostle was about to share was far from common knowledge, hence the word *mystery*. Understandably, this exceptional declaration from the apostle Paul holds one of the main keys to understanding the context for the return of Jesus Christ.

In the school of prophetic understanding, it is understood that the rapture of the Church and the second coming of Jesus Christ are two different events and are not to be confused. Therefore, the return of Jesus Christ must be viewed in the context of two separate occurrences in which He will:

A) Take away (rapture) believers from the earth as impending judgment is about to come. In this return, the Lord will not set foot directly on the earth, but rather He will descend in the heavens, in the air, where He will resurrect all dead saints, and those who are alive at that time will be changed and be caught up together to meet Him in the clouds (1 Thess. 4:15–17).

B) Put an end to all evil, set up His eternal kingdom, and reign on the earth. In this ultimate second homecoming, the Lord literally returns to earth with His saints, (during Armageddon), and His feet will touch the Mount of Olives, causing it to split in two from east to west (Zech.14).

Yes, Jesus did say, "But of that day and hour no one knows, not even the angels of heaven, but My Father only" (Matt. 24:36). However, is it possible that this scripture has been misinterpreted? To isolate this scripture and to just take it at face value is to not rightly divide the word of truth (2 Tim. 2:15). The Bible also says, for example, "Surely the Lord God does nothing, unless *He reveals His secret* to His servants the prophets" (Amos 3:7). Could this scripture have anything to do with the apostle Paul saying, "Behold I tell you a *mystery*" (1 Cor. 15:51), a secret?

Is it the ultimate plan of the Lord Jesus Christ for His return to be kept a secret, and if so, what are the pros and cons? Would there be any difference if we were to know when His return will be? Jesus said we would know when His return is imminent, even at the door. Normally we know when someone is at the door because of a knock, the sound of the doorbell, etc.

This book goes contrary to the belief and understanding of many; but I do believe, based on the scriptures, that the return of Jesus Christ will fit into a specific time frame—though it will be by no means predictable to the very day. We are told through the scriptures, for example, that the second coming of Jesus Christ will take place in the days of the ten kings (or kingdoms) of Daniel 2:4–46 and the battle of Armageddon in Revelation 19. The scriptures also indicate that this battle will take place at the ending of the final seven years of the tribulation period.

Therefore, it is not outrageous and/or unbiblical to foresee the second coming of Jesus. What we are not able to do, however, is to predict when exactly the Antichrist will appear on the world's scene to orchestrate and sign a peace deal with Israel that will initiate those final seven years of Daniel's seventieth week prophetic period. But once the seven-year period begins, then we have ourselves a context, not only for Armageddon and many other events but also for the ultimate return of Jesus. In like manner, no one can predict the day or precise timing when Jesus will return for the saints in the rapture, but it too has a specific and unique context.

There are many other end-time prophecies that correspond with the return of Jesus, and this book will highlight some of those events that will undoubtedly be signs of conviction and reassurance to the faithfulness of God's word and promises. Jesus did in fact say there would be signs both preceding and setting the stage for His return, and we would know when it is near (Matt. 24).

My aim in this book is to make clearer and better understood prophetic scriptures as they relate to the end times and the more plainly defined time (context) of the return of Jesus Christ, both for the rapture and ultimately for His second coming to rule and reign on the earth. We are about to see, through scripture, that the return of Jesus Christ as prophesied is much clearer than we thought or maybe have been taught.

While this book focuses a lot on prophecies related to the return of Jesus with a wealth of scriptures, as you read this book, you will also find within its pages a clear caution and warning to not be a "signs watcher." At times, we put off important and life-changing decisions because of the idea that we have lots of time or a certain prophecy hasn't been fulfilled yet. But certain things, especially those of eternal significance, should not be placed on the back burner of our lives while we're focusing primarily on the fulfillment of prophecy and giving no serious thought and effort to the lives we live, as each day could be our very last. So let us make the most out of life, fulfilling the purposes for which God has created us.

CHAPTER 1

THE RETURN OF JESUS FOR THE RAPTURE AND ITS TIMING

The concept of the rapture is nothing new in terms of biblical experiences. Throughout the scriptures we've seen God at work delivering or protecting His people or individuals from various trials and tribulations. Since God has a faithful track record of being true to His word, there is no reason why we should doubt His promise of such a miraculous exodus from earth for those who live and put their faith in Him.

Jesus said in John 14:1–3:

> Let not your heart be troubled, you believe in God, believe also in Me. In My Father's house there are many mansions; if it were not so, I would have told you. I go to prepare a place for you. And if I go and prepare a place for you, I will come again and receive you to Myself; that where I am, there you may be also.

This is one of the greatest promises to the believer; Jesus will indeed return. Not only will Jesus return, but He's also coming back to fulfill this specific promise. This event, the rapture, is when all the true saints (believers) who have died, all the way back to Adam, will be resurrected to life, and those who are alive at that time will be caught up together to meet the Lord Jesus Christ in the air. God will escort us into His eternal presence in heaven.

For those who believe, the scripture puts it this way in the context of losing a loved one, and for those who have no hope:

> I do not want you to be ignorant, brethren, concerning those who have fallen asleep, lest you sorrow as others who have no hope. For we believe that Jesus died and rose again, even so God will bring with Him those who sleep in Christ. For this we say to you by the word of the Lord, that we who are alive and remain until the coming of the Lord will by no means precede those who are asleep. For the Lord Himself will descend from heaven with a shout, with the voice of an archangel, and with the trumpet of God. And the dead in Christ will rise first. Then we who are alive and remain shall be caught up together with them in the clouds to meet the Lord in the air. And thus we shall always be with the Lord. Therefore comfort one another with these words (1 Thess. 4:13–18).

As soon as someone makes a reference to a timeline for the return of Jesus Christ and/or the end of the world, a red flag goes up in people's minds—and to a reasonable degree, rightly so. Why? Simply because there have been more than enough false prophets who have declared a specific date for the return of Jesus Christ or the end of the world, and they have been proven wrong every time.

A red flag goes up because we have read and heard countless times, "No man knows the day or the hour," a frequent reference to Matthew 24:36. Unfortunately, this is one of the main scriptures that deals with the return of Jesus Christ that is taken out of context and misinterpreted by a vast majority. In addition, there are other scriptures, which I'll expound upon later, that must be taken into consideration when looking at Matthew 24:36.

Let's take a closer look at what Jesus said and what He meant when He said it: "But of that day and hour no one knows, not even the angels of heaven, but My Father only." The key word in this text that most people base their understanding of the return of Jesus on is the word *knows* or *knoweth*.

The word *knoweth* (KJV) is *eidos* in the Greek (1492), which means, "*to perceive with the outward senses*, particular with physical sight; to perceive with the mind."[1] If this is what the word *knoweth* means, then certainly no one knows or will know.

However, in relation to this specific scripture, Jesus didn't say it's altogether impossible to know at the present moment or at any other time in the future more insight about His return. What He meant is that it's impossible to know by or through human means. We can conclude this is a fair understanding since it is God through the Holy Spirit or His angels who are the revealer of heaven's secrets to His saints.

After the Pharisees and the Sadducees came to test Jesus and asked Him for a sign from heaven, Jesus responded,

> "When it is evening you say, 'It will be fair weather, for the sky is red'; And in the morning, 'It will be foul weather today, for the sky is red and threatening.' Hypocrites! You know how to discern the face of the sky, but you cannot discern the signs of the times" (Matt. 16:2–3).

The apostle Peter shed more light on this truth when he said, "Knowing this first, that no prophecy of scripture is of any private interpretation, for prophecy never came by the will of man, but holy men of God spoke as they were moved by the Holy Spirit" (2 Pet. 1:20–21).

If Jesus did not dismiss the possibility of ever knowing more specific details about His return, then who said we cannot know or will never know? Jesus said to His disciples:

---

[1] Zodhiated, Spiros. *The Complete Word Study New Testament: Bringing The Original Text to Life*. (Chattanooga, TN. AMG Publishers, 1991), pg. 908.

3

> *"I still have many things to say to you*, but you cannot bear them now. However, when He, the Spirit of truth, has come, He will guide you into all truth; for He will not speak on His own authority, but whatever He hears He will speak; and *He will tell you things to come"* (John 16:12–13).

Is it possible that after Jesus went back to heaven and the Holy Spirit was sent, more insight of His return was revealed to His servants? I believe so, especially because He did not say we will never know through the divine revelation of His Spirit—when as yet much more was to be revealed and declared to His saints. We can see this through the revelations given to Paul in the Pauline epistles and the other writings of the New Testament, including the book of Revelation.

It is also without question that there are many other scripture references that would indicate the return of Jesus Christ to be a surprise. Jesus spoke of the ten virgins, of whom five were ready and five weren't, saying, "Watch therefore, for you *know* neither the day nor the hour in which the Son of Man is coming" (Matt. 25:13). He also spoke about how the owner of a house, if he knew at what point in time his house would be broken into, would've stood watch and not allowed such evil to happen (Matt. 24:42–44).

Throughout this book, I will, as did Jesus, stress the importance of being a faithful servant who is always ready. Should his master make an unscheduled appearance, he won't be caught off guard, and neither will his master be disappointed in him. This is the underlying truth that Jesus was trying to convey when making numerous references to His coming at a time when we're not aware.

> "Who then is a *faithful and wise* servant, whom his master made ruler over his household, to give them food in due season? Blessed is that servant whom his master, when he comes, will find *so doing*. Assuredly, I say to you that he will make him ruler over all his goods. But *if that evil servant says in his heart, 'My master is delaying his*

coming,' and begins to beat his fellow servants, and to *eat and drink with the drunkards,* the master of that servant will come on a day when he is not looking for him and at an hour that he is not aware of, and will cut him in two and *appoint him his portion with the hypocrites.* There will be weeping and gnashing of teeth" (Matt. 24:45–51).

We're not saved just to go to heaven in the rapture. If that were the case, as soon as we accepted Jesus, He would either cause us to die and immediately be present with the Lord in spirit or be taken up into heaven like Elijah. Jesus Christ is looking for faithful servants to fulfill their God-given purpose and destinies, and to carry out the mandate of the Great Commission. If our plan is to do our own thing as the evil servant did, then God will appoint us a portion with the hypocrites—because we were fakes—just wanting to escape God's judgment, but had no true love for the Lord or desire to surrender our lives to Him.

If knowing the time frame of the return of Jesus Christ is a disadvantage, because it will cause some saints to "slack off," then would it be a "good disadvantage"? If knowing a time frame causes believers to indulge in their own desires and sinful pleasures, then it's worth asking the question, "Were they really saved, and if so, what was their motivation for living and maintaining a pure and holy life or not?"

First John 3:2–3 says, "Beloved, now we are children of God; and it has not yet been revealed what we shall be, but we know that when He is revealed, we shall be like Him, for we shall see Him as He is. And everyone who has this hope in Him purifies himself, just as He is pure."

This may in fact be an advantage on God's part. He'll know even more (though He's omniscient and knows all things perfectly) those who were truly Christlike in every area of their lives, with pure motives day in and day out. They will truly stand out. Faithful servants don't give "eye service."

In terms of the return of Jesus Christ to rapture the Church away, the scriptures indicate a context and a specific event that must take place before He returns. This is not my opinion. Many Christians believe there are no specific signs or events that must take place before Jesus returns. But my understanding in this regard is based on the scripture and is not a subjective opinion but rather a scriptural declaration:

> "Now brethren, *concerning the coming of our Lord Jesus Christ and our gathering together to Him,* we ask you not to be soon shaken in mind or troubled either by spirit of by word or by letter, as if from us, as though the day of Christ had already come. Let no one deceive you by any means; *for that Day will not come unless the falling away comes first and the man of sin is revealed,* the son of perdition, who opposes and exalts himself above all that is called God or that is worshiped, so that *he sits as God in the temple of God, showing himself that he is God.* Do you remember that when I was still with you I told you these things? And now you know what is restraining, that he may be revealed in his own time. For the mystery of lawlessness is already at work; only He who now restrains will do so until He is taken out of the way. And then the lawless one will be revealed, whom the Lord will consume with the breath of His mouth and destroy with the brightness of Him coming" (2 Thess. 2:1–8).

Has this scripture been ignored, overlooked, or simply misinterpreted by end-time prophecy enthusiasts? How does one explain away, "for that Day *will not come unless*"? Whatever the case or reasoning, this scripture is straightforward and to the point.

There are a few things in this passage of scripture to zoom in on, some of which I will address in later chapters. The Thessalonians were terrified of the thought that Jesus Christ had returned and somehow they were left behind and were going through persecution/ the great tribulation when Paul's previous teaching (1 Thess. 4:14–18) said they would be gathered together to be with the Lord. False teaching had made its way into the church, maybe through someone pretending he was sent by the apostles or through forging a letter as though it came from them. Paul made it clear that such teaching should be rejected.

Notice Paul's clear reference to the "coming of our Lord ... our gathering together with Him." He is no doubt alluding to the rapture of the Church as recorded in 1 Thessalonians 4. It is difficult to conclude otherwise since the second return of Jesus Christ (not the rapture), when He comes in wrath, riding on the white horse of Revelation 19, is clearly to destroy the Antichrist and set up His thousand-year reign. The gathering of the believers is not the initial primary focus. It is also clear that there will indeed be another gathering of the covenant people of Israel along with those who would've died during the tribulation and those who somehow may have survived it all, along with those who would've been born during that time.

Paul's reference to the "falling away" or "rebellion" in the KJV occurring first as a sign that will precede the return of Christ is worth noting.

> The term rebellion (apostasia) denotes a falling away or apostasy; and for Paul to label it simply as "the rebellion" lends credence to the notion that it is a technical term given to an expected falling away of unprecedented proportions. In his lengthy discussion of the signs pointing to the end of the age Jesus says, "At that time many will turn away from the faith and will betray and hate each other" (Matt. 24:10). Some years later, Paul, writing to Timothy, lists a number of fruits of rebellion or ungodliness that will mark the last days (2 Tim. 3:1–5).[2]

---

[2]   Arrington, French L. & Strongstad, Roger. *Full Life Bible Commentary to The New Testament, An International Commentary for Spirit-Filled Christians.* (Grand Rapids, MI. Zondervan Publishing House, 1999), pg. 1206, 1207.

French L. Arrington and Roger Stronstad believe that this falling away will be like nothing Christianity has ever seen. If we but only look around us, especially in the church of North America, we can concur that yes indeed, many are falling away from the faith as church doors close and pastors abandon the ministry. There seems to be a trend where countless people no longer want anything to do with the Church or Christianity. Then there are those who are still in the Church (or so they say) but who only have a "form of godliness, but deny its power" (2 Tim. 3:5).

I believe 2 Thessalonians 2 clearly indicates that the Church will recognize the Antichrist, though the world and/or Israel will not—until it's too late. One of the reasons for this is that the Antichrist's true colors and intentions will not be revealed immediately as he steps on the world scene. A matter of fact, he will be loved by many. Nonetheless, he is the one person who is destined to accomplish a peace deal with Israel and the Palestinians/Arabs for seven years, and that's one of the unique accomplishments that will set him apart.

Also, either the Jewish temple will be built shortly before he comes on the scene, or he'll be the one to broker the deal to have it rebuilt. Either way, there has to be, must be, a rebuilt Jewish temple in Israel on the Temple Mount. Why? Because even Jesus alluded to this specific end-time prophecy as also stated by Daniel in 11:31. Jesus said, "When you see the 'abomination of desolation' spoken of by Daniel the prophet, *standing in the holy place* (whoever reads, let him understand), then let those who are in Judea flee to the mountains" (Matt. 24:15–22).

There must be a temple for the Antichrist to "stand in the holy place" and declare himself to be God. This is the "abomination of desolation." The Antichrist is initially a man of peace who will temporarily accomplish what every American president and many other world leaders have tried and failed to do.

In specific reference to the rapture, scriptures indicate that we will not or should not be taken off guard for this grand event. The apostle Paul, after he had just spoken regarding the coming of Jesus

Christ to snatch away the saints, soon followed up this affirmation by saying:

> "But concerning the *times and the seasons*, brethren, you have no need that I should write to you. For you yourselves know perfectly that *the day of the Lord so comes as a thief in the night.* For when they say, "Peace and safety!" then sudden destruction comes upon *them*, as labor pains upon a pregnant woman. And they shall not escape. *But you brethren, are not in darkness, so that this Day should overtake you as a thief. You are all sons of light and sons of the day.* We are not of the night nor of darkness. Therefore let us not sleep, as others do, but let us watch and be sober" (1 Thess. 5:1–6).

What is interesting to note from this scripture is that Paul seems to put this event of the day of the Lord in the context or time frame of, "When they say peace and safety." The "they" in this passage is a reference to Paul's Jewish brethren, the nation of Israel of whom Daniel 9's peace deal pertains.

The return of Jesus Christ will no doubt come as a thief in the night, but this is in relation to the unbelievers. If you notice, the apostle Paul made a clear distinction between "they" and "you brethren." As much as the return of Jesus Christ will be a surprise to many as a thief in the night, it should not be so for the believer.

Matthew 16:1–4 reveals how Jesus was disappointed with the religious leaders for not knowing the signs of the times. They could judge and discern the atmospheric signs of the clouds and so forth to determine what the day was going to be like, but they failed to discern spiritual and prophetic signs regarding the coming of their Messiah.

From Jesus' point of view, they should not have missed the prophetic times they were in, since the scriptures clearly point to this grand event. If there was not enough available for them to know and discern the time, Jesus would have no grounds on which to be angry with them. They should not have been in darkness.

Now that we're looking back at the first coming of Christ from a historical point of view, it may be easy for us to say, "Wow, how could they miss that? If they had put all the prophecies together, they would've certainly known and recognized the timeline of Christ's coming and spotted Him in their midst." But just like the people of Jesus' day who had troves of prophecy at their disposal, we, who have an even greater wealth of prophetic scriptures, also may find ourselves being totally unaware of the timing of His return if we fail to understand that God has revealed His secrets to us through His word, that we should not be like those who are in darkness.

"Surely the Lord God does nothing unless He reveals His secret to His servants the prophets" (Amos 3:7). Here's an example of what the Lord meant when He said that. The Lord had visited Abraham and Sarah to reaffirm that they would have a child. Then as the Lord and the angels were departing to go and destroy Sodom and Gomorrah, the Lord said, "Shall I hide from Abraham what I am doing, since Abraham shall surely become a great and mighty nation, and all the nations of the earth shall be blessed in him? For I have known him, in order that he may command his children and his household after him, that they keep the way of the Lord" (Gen. 18:17–19). God did not hide from Abraham what He was doing.

Consider for example the story of Noah and the flood, one of the events to which Jesus compares His return. The Lord told Noah that He was about to destroy the earth and everything that moved on the face of the earth. Thus, because Noah and his family was righteous and found grace in the eyes of the Lord, the Lord told him to build an ark for himself and his family and big enough to accommodate two of every beast of the field and birds of the air. After spending over 120 years building the ark and preaching to the ungodly throughout that time, it finally came time for the Lord to act on His promise.

"Then the Lord said to Noah, 'Come into the Ark you and all your household, because I have seen that you are righteous before

Me in this generation ... *For after seven more days I will cause it to rain* on the earth" (Gen. 7:1–4). Though Noah did not know the exact time from the onset of the instruction to build the art because of the impending flood, when it got close, and at the appropriate time, God did in fact tell Noah that the rain would start after seven more days.

In the context of this story as it relates to the comparison of Jesus' return, and also that of Sodom and Gomorrah, we see that Noah was fully aware of *when looming judgment* was coming and *when his deliverance* was about to begin. God did not tell him how many years it would take and when exactly it would happen in terms of a specific year, month, or day. Nonetheless, the ungodly who did not believe but who were mocking Noah all perished because the flood *took them by surprise.* Likewise, in the case of Sodom and Gomorrah, righteous Lot was divinely warned and delivered and was not caught off guard with the immoral inhabitants of the city (See Genesis 19).

God always makes a distinction between the righteous and unrighteous. He protects His people and has bound Himself to such assurance and deliverance continuously throughout His word. The two greatest events of destruction and deliverance in the Bible are examples of God informing and covering His people while keeping the ungodly in the dark.

This scripture is of particular interest when addressing the secrets of God:

> "But as it is written: 'eye has not seen, nor ear heard, nor have entered into the heart of man the things which God has prepared for those who love Him.' *But God has revealed them to us through His Spirit. For the Spirit searches all things, yes, the deep things of God.* For what man knows the things of a man except the spirit of the man which is in him? Even so *no one knows the things of God except the Spirit of God.* Now we have received not the spirit of the world, but the Spirit who is from God, that we might know the things that have been freely given to us by God" (1 Cor. 2:9–12).

Countless times I've heard numerous people quoting this scripture, "eye has not seen," and for some reason, they choose not to continue to verse 10, which refers to the fact that God has revealed those things to us by His Spirit. It is true that "no eye has seen," but it's just as true that the Spirit of God reveals the secrets of God. On our own it's impossible to discern the workings and timing of God, but the apostle Paul, for example, stepped into such glorious revelation that very few, if any, had ever experienced and was able to share things dear to the heart of God.

One of the big misunderstandings in addressing the rapture is from a revelation given by the apostle Paul in 1 Corinthians 15. Here Paul was speaking about the resurrection of Jesus Christ and the coming resurrection of the believer. He said,

> "Behold, *I tell you a mystery*: We shall not all sleep, but we shall all *be changed—in a moment, in the twinkling of an eye, at the last trumpet.* For the trumpet will sound, and the dead will be raised incorruptible, and we shall be changed" (vv. 50–52).

The apostle Paul is letting us in on some revelation that was not everyday knowledge, hence the term *mystery*. He did not say we will be caught up into heaven in the twinkling of an eye as numerous end-time movies portray people disappearing in the blink of an eye. It said we shall be *"changed—in a moment in the twinkling of an eye."* This miraculous change from mortal to immortality is what takes place in the twinkling of an eye, not the rapture itself.

I believe it's safe to say that over 90 percent of believers and end-time prophecy teachers, teaching on eschatology, believe that the rapture is an event in which the saints will suddenly disappear. Christian pilots, truck/car drivers, machine operators, and any and all other fields of employment or leisure activities that the saints may be involved in will be suddenly left vacant, and this will cause immediate worldwide pandemonium! But regardless of whether this event will happen in the "twinkling of an eye" or in real time, the world will certainly never be the same, and chaos is sure to follow.

As for the actual timing or speed of the rapture itself, we have no clear indication from scripture in this regard. However, every event in the Bible of a believer going to heaven, except for a lack of information on the part of Enoch, was in real time and in visible sight by onlookers. Elisha saw Elijah going up (2 Kings 2); the disciples saw Jesus returning to heaven (Acts 1:4–11); and the whole world will watch the two witnesses of Revelation 11 ascending back up to heaven.

Interestingly, the timing of the rapture is revealed through the mystery of the revelations given to the apostle Paul by Jesus Christ in 2 Corinthians 12:1–10. It is at the last trumpet. When shall we be changed from mortal to immortality? "We shall all be changed—in a moment in the twinkling of an eye, *at the last trumpet*" (1 Cor. 15:51, 52). This "at" indicates both a timing and a context. Believers will be changed from mortal to immortality and be raptured in the context of or a set/series of trumpets being sounded. The "last" means there is more than one, and this change/event all happens at the "last trumpet."

One thing we should keep in mind when focusing on the revelatory insights of the apostle Paul, as briefly mentioned before, is that he was caught up to the third heaven, saw, and heard things that none of the other apostles or believers were privy to, except for maybe John. So great was the insight and revelation that he said it is "not lawful for a man to utter" (2 Cor. 12:4). He had many reasons to boast above his contemporaries because God let him in on some of His "top secrets."

The apostle Paul was an "outsider." He was rejected by the other apostles and Church brethren because of his record as a persecutor of the Church. Many were in fear of him, and after his conversion on the road to Damascus, they questioned his sincerity and were reserved in accepting him. He had to "prove" himself. He was the only one among the elites who had not walked with Jesus. However, he met Jesus on the road to Damascus and was taught the gospel through divine revelation (Gal. 1:10–12).

So this "last trumpet" is key to understanding not only the context but also the timeline of the rapture. Should there be some doubt concerning the apostle Paul's reference to the last trumpet and how it ties in with the timeline of the rapture, there is also an angelic host who gave specific emphasis and attention to the last trumpet—affirming and confirming what Paul had already declared.

In Revelation 10, the angel of the Lord made an emphatic proclamation. John begins this passage by saying,

> "The angel whom I saw standing on the sea and on the land raised up his hand and swore by Him who lives forever and ever, who created heaven and the things that are in it, the earth and the things that are in it, and the sea and the things that are in it, that there should be delay no longer, but *in the days of the sounding of the* **seventh angel**, *when he is about to* **sound**, *the* **mystery of God** *would be* **finished**, as He declared to His servants the prophets" (vv. 5–7).

If I were to put together only the words in boldface in the above scripture, it would read like this: "Seventh angel sound, mystery of God finished."

This opens a new phase of questions and understanding. What exactly is the mystery of God—the mystery that would be finished at the sounding of the seventh trumpet angel? Well, in short, it is the Church, the Gentiles being grafted into the olive tree of Israel. I will further expound on this profound truth in a later chapter.

I have thus established a basic foundation to put certain scriptures together in a more understandable way. It would be very difficult to just address the timing of the return of Jesus Christ for the rapture without knowing the purpose of the rapture and the context into which it fits.

At face value, no one can predict when Jesus Christ will return, but with this context that I will further set out to establish and define, we'll see that prophecy reveals the time frame of His return. There are those who believe there are no specific prophetic sign(s) and event(s) that must first take place but that Jesus can simply return at any given moment. I disagree. I believe the scriptures teaches otherwise. Let's journey ...

CHAPTER 2

WE ARE NOT APPOINTED UNTO GOD'S WRATH

The wrath of God is one of the main reasons, if not the main reason, why many believers, even scholars, misunderstand the return of Jesus Christ as a mysterious event and beyond all predictability, while at the same time trying to reconcile it within a context that heralds the rapture, thus giving way for the wrath of God to come. This is done because the rapture of the Church and the wrath of God are closely related. Though according to scripture, it is very clear that the rapture will take place before the wrath of God is poured out on the earth; it is the timing, the context, and the duration of this time period of wrath and tribulation that has many somewhat confused.

There are two main reasons for the rapture: (1) God is delivering the saints from His wrath that is about to be poured out on the earth; and (2) to bring about the close of the time of the Gentiles, and to refocus His attention on the chosen Jewish nation of Israel. I will expound more on this in the next chapter.

Since I'll be dealing with the wrath of God throughout this chapter, let us examine what it actually is. The Greek defines anger/wrath with two basic understandings. (1) *"Thumos"* (2372): which means "To move impetuously, particularly as the air or wind; a violent motion or passion of the mind."[3] "This expression of wrath is applicable to both God and man. It is, however, also found with another word that is another form of wrath: "*Orge*" (3709). This form means, 'To desire eagerly or earnestly. Wrath, anger as a state of mind. Contrast Thumos, indignation, wrath as an outburst of that state of mind with the purpose of revenge.'"[4] Many times throughout the Bible, the Lord expressed His anger in various ways upon individuals and nations, but the depths of the wrath of God that is reserved for the end of times is a state of mind—not just a momentary expression of anger.

This is the wrathful state of mind that the Lord has promised to deliver His people from. First Thessalonians 1:9–10 says,

> "For they themselves declare concerning us what manner of entry we had to you, and how you turned to God from idols to serve the living and true God, and to wait for His Son from heaven, whom He raised from the dead, even Jesus who *delivers us from the wrath to come.*"

God is and has always been a gracious God, "not willing that any should perish but that all should come to repentance" (2 Pet. 3:9), but there is a time for everything.

I once heard a minister teaching on the last days who said, "Believers ought not to think that they're gonna escape this time of judgment." Well, it's not what we think; it's what the Bible says. In the case of the great flood, God protected Noah and his family; in the case of the destruction of Sodom and Gomorrah, God delivered righteous Lot and his family; and in the case of the Israelites in Egypt, God supernaturally protected the Israelites in Goshen while the rest of mainland Egypt was devastated.

---

[3] Zodhiates, Spiros. *The Complete Word Study New Testament: Bringing The Original Text to Life,* (Chattanooga, TN. AMG Publishers, 1991), pg. 922, 941.

[4] Ibib, pg. 941

This scripture indeed puts it much clearer:

> For if God did not spare the angels who sinned, but cast them down to hell and delivered them into chains of darkness, to be reserved for judgment; and did not spare the ancient world, but saved Noah, one of eight people, a preacher of righteousness, bringing the flood on the world of the ungodly; and turning the cities of Sodom and Gomorrah into ashes, condemned them to destruction, making them an example to those who afterward would live ungodly; and delivered righteous Lot … then the Lord knows how to deliver the godly out of temptations and to reserve the unjust under punishment for the day of judgment (2 Pet. 2:4–9).

God's wrath in the last days is not entirely what many people have concluded it to be. God clearly will intend for some events to be as signs to those who are watching and eagerly awaiting His coming; but others may view them as the actual wrath of God. God's wrath is not the seven seals of Revelation; and it's not within the seven trumpets. The wrath of God finds its ultimate expression within the seven bowls of Revelation 16.

Understandably, it's easy to view the disastrous events of the seven seals, seven trumpets, and seven bowls as the combined wrath of God. The reason it will be natural to conclude that these events are in fact the wrath of God, is because the world up until this point had not seen such continuous and ever-increasing in magnitude, destruction of natural, man-made and of divine nature. However, much of these disasters ought to be seen as a prelude, minor contractions before the full blow labor pains of a pregnant woman about to give birth—meteorically speaking.

There is nowhere in the book of Revelation, in reference to the seven seals or trumpets, that there is any clear declaration from heaven that these expressions of God's displeasure are a result of the depth of His wrath.

These apocalyptic acts from God are so evident to man that they cannot and will not attribute them to global warming, but instead, they will see these things as divine acts of God.

> "And the kings of the earth, the great men, the rich men, the commanders, the mighty men, every slave and every free man, hid themselves in the caves and in the rocks of the mountains, and said to the mountains and rocks, "Fall on us and hide us from the face of Him who sits on the throne and from the wrath of the Lamb! For the great day of His wrath has come, and who is able to stand?" (Rev. 6:15–17).

Even though those who are dwelling on the earth will conclude these acts to be the wrath of God, this assessment is only from their perspective. They haven't seen nothing yet in terms of what's about to unfold!

There may in fact be a subtle plan of the devil to promote the agenda and characterization of global warming behind any and every form of catastrophic natural disaster on our planet. Scientist and politicians are pointing all fingers to global warming, and in some cases, the temptation is there to politicize and/or to use such concerns for various gains. The attention/blame is then turned back to the citizens of our world as the ones who are destroying the planet (for example, the ozone layer) and making us vulnerable to countless disasters and side effects.

The downside to this view is that we run the risk of blaming everything on humans and our way of life. By constantly doing this, it's very possibly to miss the divine orchestration of God's involvement, who often causes and directs natural occurrences as a means of signs or a message. One of these examples may easily be the sun's increased heat to scorch men, which will result in an increase of skin cancer and people dying from the effects of the sun's heat. An event like this can and may no doubt be ascribed to the depletion of our ozone layer because of all the toxic smog we've been producing—simply put, global warming. However, there is a divine/spiritual element behind it all. Revelation 16:8 speaks of an angel who was commanded to go and pour out his bowl upon the sun, which caused the sun's heat to intensify and scorch men severely.

In-depth study of Revelation will reveal that many of the apocalyptic events are clearly not the wrath of God, but more so God trying to send a message, to get humans' attention and so they will repent. This can be seen in the frequent phrase: "And they did not repent" (Rev. 9:20–21; 16:9, 11).

Believers weren't promised that they wouldn't witness these expressions of the "beginning of birth pains," but we were promised to be delivered from the "labor room" and time of "delivery." What exactly do I mean by all these metaphors?

When the disciples asked Jesus about His return and the signs of His coming, He said to them:

> "Take heed that you not be deceived. For many will come in My name, saying, 'I am He' ... But when you hear of wars and commotions, do not be terrified; for these things must come to pass first, but the end will not come immediately ... Nation will rise against nation, and kingdom against kingdom. And there will be great earthquakes in various places, and famines and pestilences; and there will be fearful sights and great signs from heaven ... And there will be signs in the sun, in the moon, and in the stars; and on the earth distress of nations, with perplexity, the sea and the waves roaring; men's heart failing them from fear and the expectation of those things which are coming on the earth, for the powers of the heavens will be shaken. Then they will see the Son of Man coming in a cloud with power and great glory ... So you also, *when you see these things happening*, know that the kingdom of God is near" (Luke 21:8–31).

Matthew's version of this reference of Jesus speaking about the terrible times of the last days says, "But all these things are merely the beginning of birth pangs" (Matt. 24:8 NASB). I'm convinced

Jesus wasn't talking about "everyday" wars, earthquakes, famines, etc. These are things that have always been around, but now there will be an obvious intensity and frequency (many of which will be divine in nature), and they will be much more global in scope.

I believe the Church of Jesus Christ will see a lot more than we thought we would see. However, to stress a point that I hope to keep stressing throughout this book, let me share a few more verses from the text:

> "But take heed to yourselves, lest your hearts be weighed down with carousing, drunkenness, and cares of this life, and that Day come on you unexpectedly. For it will come as a snare on all those who dwell on the face of the whole earth. Watch therefore, and pray always that you may be counted worthy to escape all these things that will come to pass, and to stand before the Son of man" (vv. 34–36).

Here again Jesus indicated that we will be delivered from this final stage of wrathful judgment on the earth. He also warns against carousing and living carelessly while "keeping one eye open," looking out for signs. Believers will see, and have already been seeing, some of these apocalyptic events as we're already living in the last days. We are only destined to see a glimpse of these things as they're meant to also be a sign to us of Christ's imminent return, but we will escape the outpouring and climax of it.

In the Old Testament book of Malachi, there was a conversation between two groups of people. One group was saying it is, "Useless to serve God; what profit is it that we have kept His ordinance, and that we have walked as mourners before the Lord of host?" (Mal. 3:14).

> "Then those who feared the Lord spoke to one another, and the Lord listened and heard them; so a book of remembrance was written before Him for those who feared the Lord and who meditate on His name. 'They shall be mine,' says the Lord of hosts, "On the day that

I make them My jewels. And I will spare them as a man spares his own son who serves him. Then you shall again discern between one who serves God and one who does not serve Him. For behold, the day is coming, burning like an oven, and all the proud, yes, all who do wickedly will be stubble. And the day which is coming shall burn them up," says the Lord of hosts, that will leave them neither root nor branch. But to you who fear My name the Sun of righteousness shall arise with healing in His wings; and you shall go out and grow fat like stall-fed calves" (3:16–4:2).

It is on these many scriptural premises that we believe Jesus Christ will return for His Church before the wrath of God is unleashed on the earth. "For God did not appoint us to wrath, but to obtain salvation through our Lord Jesus Christ" (1 Thess. 5:9). This is, I believe, one of the main reasons why students and teachers of end-time prophecy have concluded that the rapture must precede the wrath of God.

"For the wrath of God is revealed from heaven against all ungodliness and unrighteousness of men, who suppress the truth in unrighteousness … But in accordance with your hardness and your impenitent heart you are treasuring up for yourself wrath in the day of wrath and revelation of the righteous judgment of God, who will render to each one according to his deeds" (Rom. 1:18—2:11).

John the Baptist had the revelation of the wrath of God when he said to the multitude, "Brood of vipers! Who warned you to flee from the wrath to come? Therefore bear fruit worthy of repentance" (Luke 3:7–8).

"Since it is a righteous thing with God to repay with tribulation those who trouble you, and to give you who are troubled rest with us when the Lord Jesus is revealed from heaven with His mighty angels, in flaming fire taking vengeance on those who do not know God, and on those who do not obey the gospel of our Lord Jesus Christ. These shall be punished with everlasting destruction from the presence of the Lord and from the glory of His power, when He comes, in that Day, to be glorified in His saints" (2 Thess. 1:6–10).

To be an atheist, lifelong sinner, agnostic, or whatever junction in life one may find oneself, there would still be hope for any individual in this time (age) of grace as long as one is alive. "To all the living there is hope, for a living dog is better than a dead lion" (Eccles. 9:4). When we turn to a merciful God, He still has compassion and forgives. Unfortunately, as the age of grace comes to an end, so the possibility of ever being reconciled with God decreases. "For God so loved the world that He gave His only begotten Son, that whoever believes in Him should not perish but have everlasting life" (John 3:16).

Ecclesiastes 8:11–13 says,

"Because the sentence against an evil work is not executed speedily, therefore the heart of the sons of men is fully set in them to do evil. Though a sinner does evil a hundred times, and his days are prolonged, yet I surely know that it will be well with those who fear God, who fear before Him. But it will not be well with the wicked."

"God is a just judge, and God is angry with the wicked every day. If He does not turn back, He will sharpen His sword; He bends His bow and makes it ready" (Ps. 7:11–13).

The wrath of God that is yet to come is unlike anything this world has ever seen!

Now, if there is a context for the wrath of God, then there is also a context for the return of Jesus Christ for the rapture.

According to the book of Revelation, it is not until chapter 16 that the totality of God's wrath is poured out. The introduction to this unprecedented event reads: "Then I heard a loud voice from the temple saying to the seven angels, 'Go and pour out the bowls of the wrath of God on the earth'" (v. 1). This is the first and only declaration from a heavenly host that the wrath of God is now initiated.

There is also, however, another interesting event that will be unfolding in parallel form that makes this period of the wrath of God even more devastating. The devil's own wrath will be stirred up to do as much damage as he can because his days are now numbered to just three and a half years at the most.

Revelation 12 states that there was war in heaven between Michael and his angels and the dragon (Satan). Satan and his angels were cast out of heaven, and no more place was found in heaven for them. Then John said,

> "I heard a loud voice in heaven saying, 'Now salvation, and strength, and the Kingdom of our God, and the power of His Christ have come. For the accuser of our brethren, who accused them before our God day and night has been cast down. And they overcame him by the blood of the Lamb and by the word of their testimony' … Therefore rejoice O heavens, and you who dwell in them! *Woe* to the inhabitants of the earth and the sea! *For the devil has come down to you having **great wrath**, because he knows that he has a short time*" (vv. 10–13).

This battle was never really about you and me; the devil doesn't care about us or desires anything good toward us. There is nothing good in him for him to desire good. He hates God and all God has made and stands for. The Lord noting that, "It was good," in Genesis after each act of creation (Gen 1:1—2:3) is the same "good" that the devil seeks to corrupt and destroy, primarily because he hates the Creator. If he can't inflict harm to the Creator, then he'll try to do it to His creation—because doing so would ultimately hurt the Creator.

What is often overlooked in addressing and trying to understand the wrath of God, especially in the context of the great tribulation, is the part the devil plays. Many see this time as just God letting loose His vengeance, justice, and judgment on the earth. However, Satan plays a major role in this time period being defined as the great tribulation, because he's also pouring out his wrath.

Satan will be extremely furious with God, the God he tried to overthrow and who booted him out of heaven! Now he's about to take it out on humankind, particularly the Jewish nation of Israel and new converts to Christ. There will be widespread devastation on the earth like never before! This will take place in the second half of the seven-year period allotted to the final season of the end times. Since the next chapter has to do with this seven-year period along with its two divisions, and how these things and others fall into place, I will deal with Satan being cast to earth in its full context in the next chapter, along with the ramifications of such an event taking place.

"For the mystery of lawlessness is already at work. Only He who now restrains will do so until He is taken out of the way. And then the lawless one will be revealed..." (2 Thess. 2:7–8). There is coming a time when the devil will pretty much have free reign on the earth—having no power to really oppose him (though he'll always be the devil on a leash where the sovereign power of God is concerned—see the related story in the book of Job).

The "He" that this scripture is referring to is not the Church, as some may believe. Neither is it saying that when the Church is raptured and the Holy Spirit is no longer here, only then can the Antichrist be revealed. Notwithstanding, it is in reference to the Holy Spirit and/or the Holy Spirit's work in and through the believer. The Holy Spirit is omnipresent (everywhere at all times). What the scripture is saying is that the Holy Spirit's restraining power will be removed so God's leash on the devil will be extended.

The Spirit of God has to be here and must be here in order to minister graceful conviction to the last few remaining souls who will repent and turn to Jesus, even though chances are they will do so at the expense of losing their lives. It will also be the work of the Holy Spirit that turns Israel back to God and removes the veil from their eyes to accept Jesus as Messiah.

At this point in the unfolding of the end, heaven is not all that interesting in grace and mercy. After the third angel pours out his bowl on the rivers and springs of water, turning them into blood, he then turns his attention to God by saying: "You are righteous, O Lord, the One who is and who was and who is to come, because You have judged these things. For they have shed the blood of saints and prophets, and You have given them blood to drink. For it is their just due" (Rev. 16:5–6).

Just in case God was thinking twice about His wrath being poured out on earth and its inhabitants, with the thought of showing mercy, the angel was encouraging Him to "let loose" and not to hold back because humankind is deserving of His judgment and wrath. This will no doubt be a sad and next-to-hopeless time in human history!

Oftentimes we take the mercy and compassionate grace of the Lord for granted by taking advantage of it, but what will it be like when the Lord is no longer willing to extend it to humankind?

David, for example, knew how forgiving and compassionate the Lord was that he felt more comfort in letting God deal with him than he would in falling into the hands of his enemy. After David sinned, the Lord put forth three options to discipline David: (1) seven years of famine; (2) be on the run from his enemies for three months; (3) three days of plague in the land. David then said, "I am in great distress. Please let us fall into the hand of the Lord, for His mercies are great; but do not let me fall into the hand of man" (2 Sam. 24:14).

> "So it was, that the Lord sent the plague upon the land. From Dan to Beersheba seventy thousand men of the people died. And when the angel stretched out His hand over Jerusalem to destroy it, the Lord relented from the destruction, and said to the angel who was destroying the people, 'It is enough; now restrain your hand'" (vv. 15–16).

There is a time for everything, and God will eventually get to the place where He won't hold back. Isaiah 42:13–14 declares,

> "The Lord shall go forth like a mighty man; He shall stir up His zeal like a man of war. He shall cry out, yes, shout aloud; He shall prevail against His enemies. 'I have held My peace a long time, I have been still and restrained Myself. Now I will cry like a woman in labor, I will pant and gasp at once. I will lay waste the mountains and hills.'"

The wrath of God can be summed up in two categories: (1) the righteous judgment and anger of God are no longer held back by His mercy, grace, and longsuffering but is poured out in full strength. (2) God "releases" Satan, who is also full of wrath and anger toward God and humankind. These two events happening simultaneously comprises the wrath of God and the great tribulation.

This is not a time when God loses His cool and does things He'll later regret. His wrath is the full extent of His justice. The truth is, if we were in the place of God, we would've unleashed our wrathful displeasure on humankind for all their evil and the fact that rejecting God has been glamorously glorified. God is always just, even when we don't fully understand His actions.

Nonetheless, the hard truth remains that if we reject the grace and mercy of Jesus, we set ourselves up for facing a holy and perfect God in all our imperfections, and that is not something to look forward to.

CHAPTER 3

THE GREAT TRIBULATION: SEVEN YEARS OR THREE AND A HALF YEARS?

Ever since I began developing an interest in end-time prophecy, I've always heard of the great tribulation—the seven years of apocalyptic judgments from God! So to indicate that this teaching is not entirely correct might seem a bit unconventional. Careful study of the scriptures, however, does indicate that the great tribulation is indeed three and a half years.

The reason for the understanding of the seven-year tribulation period is because of a view that the seven seals are the beginning of the tribulation period. Since there is a belief that the rapture must take place before the Antichrist is revealed because the Church's influence is what is helping to restrain him, then this fact would give room for the wrath of God to begin in parallel with the seven years reign of the Antichrist.

Most people are already familiar with the phrase *the great tribulation* and have a basic understanding about it. To gain better knowledge of this important period, we must go where the prophecy was clearly given. Allow me to share this scripture in its entirety to set the stage.

After the prophet Daniel was praying and confessing the sins of his people, an angel of the Lord (Gabriel) appeared to him to give him understanding concerning the time of the end, saying,

> *"Seventy weeks are determined for your people and for your holy city,* to finish transgression, to make an end of sins, to make reconciliation for iniquity, to bring in everlasting righteousness, to seal up vision and prophecy, and to anoint the Most Holy. Know therefore and understand, that *from the going forth of the command to restore and built Jerusalem until Messiah the Prince, there shall be seven weeks and sixty-two weeks*; the streets shall be built again, and the wall, even in troublesome times. And after the sixty-two weeks Messiah shall be cut off, but not for Himself; and the people of the prince who is to come shall destroy the city and the sanctuary. The end of it shall be with a flood, and till the time of the end of the war desolations are determined. *Then he shall confirm a covenant with many for one week*; but in the middle of the week he shall bring an end to sacrifice and offering. And on the wing of abomination shall be one who makes desolate, even until the consummation, which is determined, is poured out on the desolate" (Dan. 9:24–27).

It is important to note that failure to understand the book of Daniel makes it next to impossible to comprehend the book of Revelation. Since this scripture is so important to all Christendom, I will address some key points in it, leading up to our main subject.

First of all, this prophecy of seventy weeks is specific to the nation of Israel, its Jewish people, and the city of Jerusalem. "Seventy weeks are determined for *your people* and *your holy city.*" Well that's sort of easy because Daniel was a Jew in captivity in the land of Babylon. So, when the angel said, "your people … your holy city," he was no doubt speaking about Daniel's Jewish ancestral race and his cherished city of worship, Jerusalem. Also, the prayer of confession that Daniel was praying was in accordance to the prayer of Solomon that he prayed regarding the nation of Israel pertaining to repentance and restoration, among other things. (See 2 Chronicles 6:36–40).

Second, these seventy weeks are understood in the context of one week being the equivalent of seven years, as opposed to a seven-day week period that we're familiar with based on our calendar. Further proof of this can be found in the story of Jacob working for his wife. Jacob had entered an agreement with Laban to work seven years for one of his daughters. "Now Jacob loved Rachel; so he said, 'I will serve you seven years for Rachel your younger daughter'" (Gen. 29:18).

The Bible said those seven years seemed only like a few days to Jacob because he loved Rachel so much! But in the end Jacob was deceived and was given Leah, Rachel's older sister. After confronting Laban about the deception, Laban replied to Jacob by saying, "It must not be done so in our country, to give the younger before the firstborn. Fulfill her week, and we will give you this one also for the service which you will serve with me still another seven years" (vv. 26–27). There is also the affirmation that these are seven-year periods because of the breakdown of the seventy weeks from an historical perspective.

The first breakdown of the seventy weeks starts with a command, a decree to restore and rebuild Jerusalem, where the streets will be rebuilt, and the wall—even in troublesome times. There are a few different understandings as to when this decree was given. But there are two main commands. One was by Artaxerxes to Nehemiah to return to Jerusalem and rebuild it, namely the wall (Neh. 2). The second one was given by Cyrus to rebuild the house of the Lord (Ezra 1). There may have been more decrees like that of Darius, which was just an endorsement of a previous decree (Ezra 6). Nonetheless, these two decrees are the ones that stand out.

Rebuilding the wall in troublesome times was the first seven weeks, a period of forty-nine years that was initiated by Nehemiah. Reading the book of Nehemiah brings this prophecy into the light. This period is a prophetic fulfillment that also proves that each week equals seven years.

The second breakdown follows directly after the first seven weeks (forty-nine years). "And after the sixty-two weeks Messiah shall be cut off" (v. 26). From the ending of the first seven weeks to the ending of the additional sixty-two weeks, there is no specific or significant event that was revealed to Daniel that would take place as those years unfold.

However, it was revealed to him that at the ending of the sixty-two weeks (an additional 434 years on top of the first 49 years), the most important event in human history will take place—the Messiah (Christ) will be cut off, but not for Himself. What this all means is that careful study of this particular prophecy of Daniel could have predicted the approximate timeline of the coming of the Messiah. It points out clearly that the Messiah was going to be killed—crucified. It also presents the possibility of even knowing when it would take place.

This, to the Jews, was a paradigm shift, next to blasphemy, because in their understanding, the Messiah is not supposed to die but remains forever. Jesus said to them

> "And I, if I am lifted up from the earth, will draw all peoples to Myself. This He said signifying what death He would die. The people answered Him, "We have heard from the law that the Christ remains forever; and how can you say, 'The Son of Man must be lifted up'? Who is this Son of Man?" (John 12:32–34).

Understanding the mind-set of the Jews gives us an indication as to why they missed the Messiah—Jesus.

This important prophecy of Daniel is further expounded upon in the book of Isaiah 53.

> "Surely He has borne our griefs and carried our sorrows. Yet we esteem Him stricken, smitten by God and afflicted. But He was wounded for our transgressions, He was bruised for our iniquities; the chastisement of our peace was upon Him, and by His stripes we are

healed. All we like sheep have gone astray, we have turned, everyone to his own way; and the Lord has laid on Him the iniquity of us all. He was oppressed and He was afflicted, yet He opened not His mouth; He was led as a lamb to the slaughter, and as a sheep before its shearers is silent, so He opened not His mouth. He was taken from prison and from judgment, and who will declare His generation? For *He was cut off from the land of the living*; for the transgression of My people He was stricken. And they made His grave with the wicked—but with the rich at His death, because He had done no violence, nor was any deceit found in His mouth ... When You make His soul an offering for sin ... by His knowledge My righteous servant shall justify many, for He shall bear their iniquities ... Because He poured out His soul unto death, and He was numbered with the transgressors, and He bore the sin of many, and made intercession for the transgressors" (vv. 4–12).

Jesus could not have been born at just any time, nor could He have died at just any point; He had to fit into the context of the sixty-two weeks prophecy given by Daniel. Therefore, on one occasion Jesus said, "My time is at hand" (Matt. 26:18). Everything was preplanned and preordained. Galatians 4:4–5 says, "But *when the fullness of the time had come*, God sent forth His Son, born of a woman, born under the law, to redeem those who were under the law, that we might receive the adoption as sons."

God planned this event before time began. His plan was revealed to Daniel (along with other prophets), and the time frame in human history as to when it would be fulfilled. In fact, the Lord declares, "For I am God, and there is no other; I am God, and there is none like Me, declaring the end from the beginning, and from ancient times things that are not yet done, saying, 'My counsel shall stand, and I will do all My pleasure'" (Isa. 46:9–10).

Acts 4:27–28 also says, "For truly against Your holy Servant

Jesus, whom You anointed, both Herod and Pontius Pilate, with the Gentiles and the people of Israel, were gathered together to do whatever Your hand and Your purpose determined before to be done."

Now, mathematically speaking, if those seventy weeks or 490 years were to consecutively flow right after each other, all prophecies would have come to pass already, and the Lord Jesus Christ would be here on earth overseeing the establishment of His eternal kingdom. However, where we have an interesting detour or intermission from the seventy weeks is right after the sixty-ninth week (483 years)— the crucifixion of Jesus Christ. This gave birth to the *mystery of God*, as previously mentioned.

The apostle Paul said,

> "Israel has not obtained what it seeks; but the elect have obtained it, and the rest were blinded … I say then, have they stumbled that they should fall? Certainly not! But through their fall, to provoke them to jealousy, salvation has come to the Gentiles … For if their being cast away is the reconciling of the world, what will their acceptance be but life from the dead? For if the first fruit is holy, the lump is also holy; and if the root is holy, so are the branches. And if some of the branches were broken off, and you, being a wild olive tree, were grafted in among them, and with them became a partaker of the root and fatness of the olive tree, do not boast against the branches. But if you do boast, remember that you do not support the root, but the root supports you. You will say then, 'Branches were broken off that I might be grafted in.' Well said. Because of unbelief they were broken off, and you stand by faith … For God is able to graft them in again. For if you were cut out of the olive tree which is wild by nature, and were grafted contrary to nature into a cultivated olive tree, how much more will these, who are natural branches, be grafted into their own olive tree?" (Rom. 11:11–24).

Let me say this: to those who preach and believe in "replacement theology" (meaning the Church is now the "new Israel"—the chosen, elect people of God), this is a doctrine of demons that no doubt helps to inspire anti-Semitism. God has made an eternal covenant with the Jewish nation of Israel that He has bound Himself to. (See Jeremiah 30–31). Obviously God never intended just to save the Jews. Nor was it His plan to use the Jews and the covenant promise to Abram (Gen. 12) to bless the world and then to turn around and curse them.

Those who promote this "replacement theology" are on the wrong side of history and future history. Gentiles were the ones who were strangers and foreigners from the commonwealth and citizenship of Israel, not the other way around. (See Ephesians 2:11–22).

Hank Hanegraaff, the host of *The Bible Answer Man*, in his book *The Apocalypse Code* alludes to the fact that God's intent was always for one chosen people, saying,

> "Far from communicating that God has two distinct people, the Scriptures from beginning to end reveal only one chosen people purchased 'from every tribe and tongue and language and nation' (Revelation 5:9). As Paul explains, the 'mystery is that through the gospel the Gentiles are heirs together with Israel, members together of one body, and sharers together in the promise in Christ Jesus'" (Ephesians 3:10). [5]

Jesus said to His disciples, "Blessed are the eyes which see the things you see; for I tell you that many prophets and kings have desired to see what you see, and have not seen it, and to hear what you hear, and have not heard it" (Luke 10:23–24).

---

[5]   Hanegraaff, Hank. *The apocalypse Code, Find Out What The Bible Really Days About The End Times And Why it Matters Today*, (Nashville TN. Thomas Nelson. 2007), Pg. 49.

"Of this *salvation* the prophets have inquired and searched carefully, who prophesied of the grace that would come to you, searching what manner of time, the Spirit of Christ who was in them was indicating when He testified beforehand the sufferings of Christ and the glories that would follow. To them it was revealed that, not themselves, but to us they were ministering the things which now have been reported to you through those who have preached the gospel to you by the Holy Spirit sent from heaven—things which angels desire to look into" (1 Pet. 1:10–12).

It's not so much that the redemption of the Gentiles was a mystery; it was more the way in which it happened. The Old Testament makes numerous references of God's plan to reach the Gentiles, such as Isaiah 49:6, and God did reach the Gentiles through the ministry and redemptive work of Jesus Christ. "For God was in Christ reconciling the world to Himself, not imputing their trespasses to them" (2 Cor. 5:19).

God is not a polygamist or adulterer—having the Church as one wife and then Israel as the other. God's plan was and always has been to unite us together as one, the chosen, peculiar, royal priesthood people of God. Thus we have the picture of a single tree comprised of believing Gentiles and the chosen covenant people of Israel. We also have the picture of a unified body, representing Israel and the Church—together as the bride of Christ—the elect.

This amazing plan of God was so ingeniously hidden in God through Christ that the devil thought he was doing a good thing and winning a great battle by crucifying Jesus Christ. But the word of God portrays something far beyond the understanding of such evil powers. "But we speak the wisdom of God in a mystery, the hidden wisdom which God ordained before the ages for our glory, which none of the rulers of this age knew; *for had they known, they would not have crucified the Lord of glory*" (1 Cor. 2:7–8).

The "sufferings of Christ and the glories that would follow" has all to do with those who would henceforth believe in Jesus Christ.

This scripture coincides with Hebrews 12:3, "For the joy that was set before Him, He endured the cross." This is also further supported by the prayer of Jesus in John 17:20, "I do not pray for these alone, but also for those who will believe in Me through their word."

Bill Salus in his book *Psalm 83* said,

> "Many believe that God is done with the Jew, and that the Jewish people are no longer 'My people Israel.' They believe that the Jew has no further place within the overall prophetic plan of God. They surmise that the Church has replaced them as the people of God. Estimates tell us this dangerous misconception, known as Replacement Theology, is held by as much as 85 percent of the visible Church."[6]

It is really sad when so many within the Church fail to understand the plan of God and His covenant promise to Israel and to bless the nations through them.

There are many scriptures that give a clear understanding as to what the mystery of God is, such as Romans 16:26; Colossians 1:24–27, 4:3–4; and 1 Timothy 3:16. However, there is one scripture in particular that presents this mystery in such a unique way that it's worth sharing: Ephesians 3:1–12:

> "For this reason I, Paul, the prisoner of Christ Jesus for *you Gentiles*—if indeed you have heard of the dispensation of the grace of God which was given to me for you, *how that by revelation He made known to me the mystery* (as I have briefly written already, by which, when you read, you may understand my knowledge in *the mystery of Christ*), *which in other ages was not made known to the sons of men, as it has now been revealed by the Spirit to His holy apostles and prophets: that the Gentiles should be fellow heirs, of the*

---

6   Salus, Bill. *Psalm 83: The missing Prophecy Revealed. How Israel Becomes the Next Mideast Superpower!* (La Quinta, CA. Highway, A division of Anomaslos Publishing, 2013), pg.62

same body, and partakers of His promise in Christ through the gospel, of which I became a minister according to the gift of the grace of God given to me by the effective workings of His power. To me, who am less than the least of all the saints, this grace was given, that I should preach among the Gentiles the unsearchable riches of Christ, and to make all see what is the fellowship of the mystery, which *from the beginning of the ages has been hidden in God* who created all things through Jesus Christ; to the intent *that now the manifold wisdom of God might be made known by the church* to the principalities and powers in the heavenly places, according to the eternal purpose which He accomplished in Christ Jesus our Lord."

It was this mystery—the Gentiles/Church—that the angel was referring to in Revelation 10:5–7, of which John speaks, saying,

"Then the angel whom I saw standing on the sea and on the land raised up his hand to heaven and swore by Him who lives forever and ever, who created heaven and the things that are in it, the earth and the things that are in it, and the sea and the things that are in it, that there should be delay no longer, but in the days of the *sounding of the seventh angel,* when he is about to sound, the *mystery of God would be finished,* as He declared to His servants the prophets."

This was nothing new; it was something that was already declared to God's messengers, namely Paul, but now with greater detail. It is in the writings of the apostle Paul that we are given specific insight into the glorious transformation of the believer in the rapture, precisely at the last trumpet: "We shall not all sleep, but we shall all be changed—in a moment, in the twinkling of an eye, at the last trumpet" (1 Cor. 15:51–52).

If we believe the great tribulation to be seven full years and that it begins with the opening of the seven seals and/or more specifically the rider on the white horse signing the peace deal (a reference to the four horsemen of the apocalypse, Rev. 6), then we are forced to supplement this position by placing the rapture somewhere before Revelation 6.

Thus, many have been promoting the idea of the rapture taking place in Revelation 4. This is actually the most widely accepted view. Yet, there isn't much to support this viewpoint. In fact, the main point that is addressed in proving this scripture to be the rapture is a unique event that cannot be clearly supported by other scriptures.

Let us examine this scripture: "After these things I looked, and behold, a door standing open in heaven. And the first voice which I heard was like a trumpet speaking with me, saying, '*Come up here*, and I will show you things which must take place after this'" (Rev. 4:1).

Nowhere in the Bible was John as a single individual ever used symbolically, metaphorically, figuratively, or in any other way to represent the Church as a whole. John said, "The first voice which I heard was like a trumpet *speaking to me*" (v. 1). This is a very personal reference and experience between John and a heavenly being, an angel, or the Lord Himself. The purpose and goal of this conversation is to invite/usher John (and John alone) up into heaven, specifically to show him things, (what we now know as the book of Revelation) that must take place. Notice the correlating charge in 1:19, "Write the things which you have seen, and the things which are, and the things which will take place after this."

John's focus was on the first voice (trumpet) which he heard, while 1 Corinthians 15 and Revelation 10 put the emphasis on the last trumpet. Hence, these two scriptures bear witness with each other.

Furthermore, John said, "Immediately I was in the Spirit" (2:2). Daniel also had a similar encounter with an angel in which he fainted but was revived and given prophetic revelations. (See Daniel 8:15–22). A similar event as well happened to the apostle Paul (formerly Saul) on the road to Damascus. (See Acts 9). Paul actually gives further insight as to what really happened on the road to Damascus or sometime thereafter in his journey with the

Lord where he describes the abundance of revelations that were given to him in 2 Corinthians 12. He wasn't even able to tell whether this revelation was in or out of his natural body.

This personal call to "Come up here" was also declared to the two witnesses after their death and resurrection in Revelation 11:11–12. This too was specific to the two witnesses and not to any other individual or group of people. To conclude otherwise as in Revelation 4 should definitely be considered as reading too much into the text.

Proponents of the Revelation 4 rapture hold to this belief because they say the "church is not mentioned after Revelation 4." They also point to the fact that the twenty-four elders are seen with golden crowns (a symbol suggesting they've received their rewards). This understanding comes from scriptures such as Hebrews 11:39–40, which states, "And all these, having obtained a good testimony through faith, did not receive the promise, God having provided something better for us, that they should not be made perfect apart from us."

However, do we know for a fact that these crowns seen on the heads of the twenty-four elders, that they represent the rewards to be given to all the faithful saints as described in the judgment seat setting of 1 Corinthians 3:12–15, 2 Corinthians 5:10, and 2 Timothy 4:7–8? I don't believe it's that easy to make this conclusion. Could it be possible that the twenty-four elders are the human pillars of God's new government in the New Jerusalem, that they have been given something, a crown, over and above what the rest of the saints will receive? Consider also that in Revelation 11:15–19 we see heaven being open again and this time with a more defined declaration and purpose: "Your wrath has come, and the time of the dead, that they should be judged and that You should reward Your servants the prophets and the saints, and those who fear Your name small and great" (v. 18). If the reward ceremony had already taken place in Revelation 4, then how is it that we still have the angel saying that "now is the time to reward Your servants" in Revelation 11?

Why is the Church not mentioned after Revelation 4? Our answers and interpretation may differ as we read through Revelation.

One may also ask: "Why is God not mentioned in the book of Esther?" This latter question may be considered a cheap shot out in left field and somewhat irrelevant and has no relation. The principle still remains: though God was not mentioned in Esther, He was certainly there in action. And though the word *Church* is not mentioned after Revelation 4, this is by no means an indication that the saints of God cease to exist in later chapters. Something else that is also noteworthy is that even in the second return of Jesus in Revelation 19 in which the Church would've already been raptured and now returning with Jesus, we do not see the word *Church* used again.

It was never just about the Church, the Gentiles. It was always about the people of God, the bride of Christ, the chosen people of God comprising of the covenant Jewish people and Gentiles. In fact, the Church is not the highlight of these final seven years but Israel and a world that has rejected God.

Pastor Perry Stone, a prolific preacher and well-established scholar in the end-time prophecy theater, believes otherwise. In his 2014 Prophetic Summit at OCI in Cleveland, Tennessee, Pastor Perry Stone gave a profound and in-depth exhortation on the three main positions of the precise timing of the rapture held by most believers. He spoke on the belief of post-trib, mid-trib, and pre-trib, while giving supporting and conflicting scriptures for each. I must say, however, that this is a trademark of a good teacher and good teaching. Even though he's a pre-trib believer, he still takes the time to study the entirety of God's word and to help people come to a better understanding of the scriptures, even though he, like most of us, has his own beliefs and bias when it comes to the book of Revelation.

Nonetheless, he also made a good case for mid-trib, except for the fact that the "mystery of God" was the "curveball" for him. He stated, "The mystery of God referred to by the angel of Revelation 10 is the book of Daniel that was sealed, that he (John) had to eat. But now he's commanded not to seal the book of revelation" (Perry Stone, 2014 Prophetic Summit).

In Daniel 12, the angel had told Daniel, "Shut up the words, and seal the book until the time of the end; many shall run to and fro, and knowledge shall increase" (v. 4). In Pastor Perry's understanding, "God showed John the completion of Daniel." While it is certainly true that John got a more in-depth understanding of Daniel's prophecy, even to its completion, connecting this mystery to Revelation 10 with such an interpretation cannot be fully supported by scripture.

Pastor Perry Stone even suggested, "The reason Paul never expounded on the mystery of the seventh trumpet was because the people already knew about it." However, this doesn't seem feasible. Paul was more educated than that to be calling something that is common knowledge a "mystery." Again, the apostle Paul got "top secret" revelations that none of the other disciples or apostles were privy to, and there were things he was prohibited from disclosing. That to me does indeed sounds like a secret, a mystery.

Yes, Paul may not have expounded much on the seventh trumpet because the sounding of trumpets was common knowledge for Jews in terms of the feast of trumpets. However, the fact that the angel unites the timing of the seventh trumpet to the completion of the mystery of God cannot be disputed. The mystery of God is not John getting further revelation of Daniel's prophecies.

So what is so significant about the last or seventh trumpet? Well, both the rapture of the saints and the close of the Church age become a reality. Since the seventh trumpet is of such importance, it's worth taking a closer look at what actually happens when the last of the seven trumpets is sounded.

> "Then the seventh angel sounded: and there were loud
> voices in heaven, saying, 'The kingdoms of this world
> have become the kingdoms of our Lord and of His
> Christ, and He shall reign forever and ever.' And the
> twenty four elders who sat before God on their thrones
> fell on their faces and worshipped God, saying: 'We give
> You thanks, O Lord God Almighty, the One who is and

who was and who is to come, because You have taken Your great power and reigned, the nations were angry and Your wrath has come, and the time of the dead, that they should be judged, and that You should reward your servants the prophets and the saints, and those who fear Your name, small and great, and should destroy those who destroy the earth'" (Rev. 11:15–18).

From looking carefully into this text, I believe it provides ample evidence that this indeed is the rapture in motion followed by God getting ready to unleash His wrath.

Some things to note:

- The kingdoms of this world have become the kingdoms of our Lord.
- Your (God's) wrath has come.
- The time of the dead that they should be judged.
- Time to reward the servants, the prophets and saints, and those who feared Your name.
- Time to destroy those who destroy the earth.

Judging the dead, namely God's servants, prophets, saints, and those who feared His name, is the picture we see from the judgment seat of Christ in 1 Corinthians 3:9–15 and 2 Corinthians 5:9–11. This gathering is for a specific group of people—believers. It is not a judgment of condemnation or to see if one's name is in the book of life; it's a judgment or ruling for rewards.

Notice also that special emphasis is given to the fact that God's wrath has come and that now is the time to destroy those who destroy the earth. This makes sense considering believers would need to be delivered before God starts to pour out His wrath and to destroy those who destroy the earth. It is also at this point that John saw heaven opened, possibly for the descent of Jesus to resurrect and make welcome the raptured saints.

This is one of the many areas in which Pastor Perry Stone and I are in total agreement, because he too believes that it's in Revelation 11 (where the seventh trumpet sounds) that the administration of the judgment seat of Christ occurs. It is also noteworthy to consider that the seventh trumpet sounded right in the middle of the seven years of Daniel's seventieth week, or what is widely known as the "seven years of great tribulation." If this is really the case, then it's further evidence that the Church can and more than likely will be here up until the middle of those seven years.

This period is where a lot of things come back into play, even some of the things I've briefly mentioned before. These are a few of the things that will take place in the middle of the final seven years or Daniel's seventieth week, or shortly thereafter:

- The peace treaty with Israel will be broken.
- The Antichrist will set up the abomination of desolation, declaring himself as God.
- The two witnesses will be killed and resurrected after three days and ascend back to heaven.
- War breaks out in heaven.
- Satan is cast down to the earth and is in great fury.
- Worldwide persecution of Jews begins and those who will accept Christ in those days.
- There is an outpouring of the seven bowls full of the wrath of God.
- There is enforcement of the mark of the beast.

The beginning of Israel's final seven years will not commence with terrible wars and trepidation. It starts out peacefully. "When they say peace and safety" (1 Thess. 5:3). It is not until the middle of those seven years that things really begin to get dark for the nation of Israel and for the rest of the world. This period is what the Bible also refers to as the "time of Jacobs's trouble."

Jeremiah 30:6–7 describes it this way,

> "Ask now, and see, whether a man is ever in labor with child? So why do I see every man with his hands on his lions like a woman in labor, and all faces turned pale? Alas! For that day is great, so that none is like it; and it is the time of Jacob's trouble, but he will be saved out of it."

It is hard to imagine another period in our history wherein the Jewish people will again be faced with such atrocity and plans of annihilation! This 7-year period or its more precise 3.5-year period of great tribulation is designed as a humbling and refining period specifically for Israel. We must always keep in mind that the seventy weeks (490 years) of Daniel was in relation to the Jews and their holy city. The Gentiles were a mystery that was intertwined throughout a great deal of this time period.

To further prove this point, Daniel 12:1 states, "At that time Michael shall stand up, the great Prince who stand watch over the sons of your people; and there will be a time of trouble, such as never was since there was a nation, even to that time. And at that time your people shall be delivered." It is not a coincidence that we see Michael in warfare in Revelation 12.

As Daniel inquired about this apocalyptic time coming upon his people, he said, "How long shall the fulfillment of these wonders be?" (12:6). He was told, "It shall be for a time, times, and half a time; and when the power of the holy people has been completely shattered, all these things shall be finished" (vv. 7–8). Daniel was further told, "From the time that the daily sacrifice is taken away and the abomination of desolation is set up, there shall be one thousand two hundred and ninety days. Blessed is he who waits, and comes to the one thousand three hundred and thirty-five days" (vv. 11–12).

Though there seems to be some discrepancy with the number of days (including the forty-two months the Gentiles will tread the holy city and the 2,260 sixty days given to the two witnesses to prophecy), at least one thing is clear: the sacrifices will be taken away in the middle of the seven years (Dan. 9:27). Reconciling these differences in number of days is due in part to the Jewish (lunar) calendar being different than the Western world and the possibility that some events will slightly overlap each other.

Immediately after Satan is cast out of heaven in Revelation 12–13, the rise of the beast happens. The beast was granted authority to continue for forty-two months. It was granted to him to make war with the saints (particularly of Jewish descent) and to overcome them (Rev. 13:4–7). Satan being cast down to earth in rage no doubt has a major impact on the renewed push to destroy the Jewish people.

Hank Hanegraaff, however, believes we are greatly mistaken about the last days period of tribulation as he challenges the widely accepted end-times view of Tim LaHaye who authors and produces the *Left Behind* series. Hanegraaff states,

> "Despite evidence to the contrary, LaHaye persists in dragging the seven-year tribulation into the twenty-first century and describing it as the time of Jacob's Trouble or the time of Jewish Tribulation. What he fails to disclose is the seminal fact that neither Jeremiah's reference to 'a time of trouble for Jacob' (Jeremiah 30:7) nor Jesus' reference to a time of 'great distress, unequaled from the beginning of the world until now—and never to be equaled again' (Matthew 24:21) refer to a holocaust in the twenty-first century that was precipitated by a Jewish rebellion against Jehovah in the sixth century AD. Both references incontrovertibly point to times past in which the very temple that gave Israel its theological and sociological identity was decimated. Jeremiah explicitly communicates that 'Jacob's trouble' takes place during the Babylonian exile—some six centuries before Jesus is even born! And Jesus emphatically places the time of Jewish tribulation in the first century ... In the end, there

> simply is no biblical warrant for a fatalistic preoccupation
> with a future seven-year tribulation."[7]

I find it difficult to agree with Hanegraaff. It is hard to believe the siege of Jerusalem and its later destruction along with its inhabitants being dispersed among the nations was worse than the Holocaust of our time. The Babylonians took booty from Israel and held its people captive in Babylon, while they were allowed to live almost regular lives. (See Jeremiah 29:4–14). In contrast, the holocaust of Nazi Germany under Adolf Hitler was not to take booty or to enslave, but to utterly annihilate and exterminate the Jewish race. It is said that over six million Jews perished during the Holocaust.

Sure enough, Jesus was speaking to His present-day audience regarding the impending destruction of the temple and Jerusalem being surrounded by armies; but most certainly He had to have had a distant future event of major similarities in mind as well. In fact, if Jesus had only the first century in mind, He could never have issue this decree:

> "But when you see Jerusalem surrounded by armies, then know that its desolation is near. Then let those who are in Judea flee to the Mountains, let those who are in the midst of her depart ... for these are the days of vengeance, that all things which are written may be fulfilled ... And Jerusalem will be trampled by Gentiles until the times of the Gentiles are fulfilled. And there will be signs in the sun, in the moon, and in the stars; and on the earth distress of nations, with perplexity, the sea and the waves roaring; men's hearts failing them from fear and the expectation of those things which are coming on the earth, for the powers of the heavens will be shaken. Then they will see the Son of Man coming in a cloud with power and great glory. Now when these

---

7   Hangeraaff, Hank. *The Apocalypse Code: Find Out What The Bible Really Says About The End Times And Why it Matters Today.* (Nashville, TN. Thomas Nelson. 2007). Pg. 62, 63.

things begin to happen, look up and lift up your heads,
because your redemption draws near" (Luke 21:20–28).

The context of these verses did not find their ultimate fulfillment in the first century, though Jerusalem was surrounded and the temple destroyed, among many other things. Plus, many generations have come and gone, and all things are not yet fulfilled. However, we do see a similar event prophesied to take place in the last days.

Revelation 11:1–3 says,

> "Then I was given a reed like a measuring rod. And the angel stood, saying, "Rise and measure the temple of God, the altar, and those who worship there. But leave out the court which is outside the temple, and do not measure it, for it has been given to the Gentiles. And they will tread the holy city underfoot for forty-two months. And I will give power to My two witnesses, and they will prophecy one thousand two hundred and sixty days, clothed in sackcloth."

This is most certainly not a first-century event. Nor do prophecies like Zechariah 14:1–2, which foretells God gathering the nations to battle against Jerusalem, find their ultimate fulfillment in the siege and subsequent destruction of Jerusalem by the Romans in AD 70. Though the Romans may have been comprised of different nationalities, it still falls short of today's (the last days) confederation of nations (particularly Arab nations—see Psalm 83) who are poised to "liberate" Jerusalem (even the land of Israel) from the Jews, though they will not succeed.

LaHaye is not erroneously dragging the prophetic utterances of neither Jeremiah or Jesus into the twenty-first century, or into the last days, for that matter. If anything, some of their utterances and that of other prophets as well, have dual meaning, twofold prophecy that will see similar occurrences throughout different time periods of history. By taking a closer look at the overall context itself and even historical fulfillment, this will bring about better understanding of the prophecies themselves. I will further explain and give examples of a twofold prophecy in chapter 5.

Have you ever wondered what Jesus meant when He said, "And unless those days were shortened, no flesh would be saved; but for the elect's sake those days will be shortened" (Matt. 24:22)? Interestingly enough, Jesus said this in the context of the "abomination of desolation" being set up in the temple in the middle of the seven years. He was not referring to the twenty-four-hour period in a day being shortened. He was speaking about this set prophetic time frame that deals mainly with the nation of Israel as it relates to Daniel's seventieth week.

If what is about to unfold in the second half of the seven-year period had been initiated from the beginning, the outpouring of God's full wrath; Satan being kicked out of heaven/released in full wrath; and the Antichrist's war against the saints and the mark of the beast, etc.; then would it not be fair to say, "no flesh would be saved"? Thank God this time period will be cut in half/shortened and that Michael will stand up to defend and deliver Israel—but not without them paying a great price, unfortunately.

God, again being the gracious God that He is, shortens this time of tribulation from seven years to three and a half years. This can also be supported by the fact that God sends His two witnesses to preach to Israel one last time in the first half of the seven years, to "turn the hearts of the fathers to the children and the hearts of the children to their fathers, lest I come and strike the earth with a curse" (Mal. 4:5–6).

The Bible is filled with stories of attempts to destroy Israel. Recent, modern, and future history will be no different. However, this world is about to see the fury of a God who will rise up and defend His covenant promise with the Jewish nation of Israel like never before!

The "wrath of Satan," as mentioned in chapter 2, will be amplified when Satan is cast to the earth. He will then empower the Antichrist, the false prophet, and the beast. These forces will be hard set against God and the nation of Israel. Job 1–2 gives us a preview of Satan lashing out at one man to prove a point and stick it to God. The final three and a half years of Daniel's final seven years prophecy will see Satan lashing out at the entire world. This will not be the beginning of birth pangs; this will be it!

The coming of the lawless one (the Antichrist) will be in accordance with the working of Satan, with all power, signs, and lying wonders (2 Thess. 2:9). It is my belief that the Antichrist making this drastic move or shift from being a peace envoy to a war maniac in the middle of the seven years is a result of Satan being cast to the earth in fury. It has always been Satan's goal of being God or declaring himself God; and this is exactly what the Antichrist does in the middle of the seven years, in the holiest of places. A similar event of Satan entering Judas as he set out to betray Jesus may again play out in the story of the Antichrist—the devil incarnate. (See Luke 22:1–6).

There has never been a time in the devil's existence where he has ever been this mad! Certainly he was mad when he was booted out of the third heaven, where God and all His holy angels dwell, but God didn't kick him out of the heavens entirely. He still has freedom to roam in heavens 1 and 2, and it seems he also has limited access (at God's discretion) to heaven 3, where he presented himself to God concerning Job.

(See Ephesians 6 for more info as to how the devil and his demonic hordes are the "spiritual host of wickedness in heavenly places"). Thus we understand the separations of the heavens to be: (1) earth's atmosphere—within the realm of gravity; (2) the cosmos of our universe, outer space, and all the galaxies; and (3) beyond the realm of the cosmos, outer space far above the heavens.

Satan's attempt to institute the mark of the beast (666) is more than just taking a mark of economic, security, or personal convenience. It's more than just having a cashless society and a way of identification to help prevent fraud and such. The essence of it is about allegiance and worship. "He was granted power to give breath to the image of the beast, that the image of the beast should both speak and cause as many as would not worship the image of the beast to be killed" (Rev. 13:15).

There are many who believe the book of Revelation is written in chronological order, while undoubtedly others do not. Nonetheless, I believe it's hard to conclude that these events as listed do not in fact take place at the beginning, the middle, and/or second half of the final seven years. Upon the basis of these scriptures that I've shared, along with others, I believe the great tribulation is reserved for the second half of the seven-year period—three and a half years.

CHAPTER 4

THE GRACE OF HEAVEN AND THE JUSTICE OF HELL

The grace of heaven represents God's best toward us—even though we weren't deserving of it. It signifies the profound truth that heaven only becomes a reality to us within the context of His grace. While recognizing and embracing God's invitation to heaven is encouraged to the utmost, being aware of the cost of rejecting such invitation and grace must also be brought to the limelight. The justice of hell becomes justifiable when one understands the preceding grace of heaven that can be forfeited or outright rejected

The Grace of Heaven

"For God so loved the world that He gave His only begotten Son, that whoever believes in Him should not perish but have everlasting life" (John 3:16). No doubt this is the most well-known passage of scripture in the Bible, and rightly so—because this is the essence of the gospel, the summarization of the life and ministry of Jesus Christ.

Jesus came to seek and save that which was lost (Luke 19:10). His mission was one of redemption and reconciliation through restitution. He came to reconcile us back to the Father—a relationship and fellowship that was lost in the garden of Eden with Adam and

Eve because of sin. The redemptive grace of God was determined to right the wrong of Adam and Eve and so bring us back into fellowship with the Father.

Jesus said in John 14:1–3:

> "Let not your heart be troubled; you believe in God, believe also in Me. In My Father's house are many mansions, if it were not so, I would have told you. I go to prepare a place for you. And if I go and prepare a place for you, I will come again and receive you to Myself; that where I am there you may be also."

This is an amazing promise to every believer. An eternity with God awaits all those who put their trust in Him. In fact, 1 John. 3:2–3 takes it a step further by saying,

> "Beloved, now we are children of God; and it has not yet been revealed what we shall be, but we know that when He is revealed, we shall be like Him, for we shall see Him as He is. And everyone who has this hope in Him purifies himself, just as He is pure."

God could've easily given us what we deserved, wrath and justice. Instead He showed us unconditional love. He gave us mercy and showed us grace to the end, that we might live in Him and with Him and not perish apart from Him. The scripture says, "God was in Christ reconciling the world to Himself, not imputing their trespasses to them ... for He made Him who knew no sin to be sin for us, that we might become the righteousness of God in Him" (2 Cor. 5:19, 21).

Heaven in the sky as we know it will be temporary. For those who have gone on to be with the Lord in bygone years, they will have a longer stay and experience in heaven; but if we remain alive up until the rapture, we'll have anywhere between three and a half years to a maximum of seven years there (depending on your view of the tribulation period) before we return with the Lord in Revelation 19. From which point we will rule and reign with the Lord on the earth.

Often when people make references to heaven, they usually do so with the idea of heaven being a place, particularly some utopia in the galaxies above. While that may be true in so many ways, heaven must also be understood not just as a place but as a state, an altogether new environment and atmosphere. It is a state in which God will tabernacle with humankind, and we will be with Him for all eternity.

> "Behold the tabernacle of God is with men, and He will dwell with them, and they shall be His people. God Himself will be with them and be their God. And God will wipe away every tear from their eyes; there shall be no more death, nor sorrow, nor crying. There shall be no more pain, for the former things have passed away ... 'Behold I make all things new'" (Rev. 21:3–5).

This will be the new environment that will be ordained and created by God in the new age to come. Much of what we do not yet know or understand will easily be grasped. The apostle Paul said that we only know in part, but when that which is perfect has come, then that which is in part will be done away with (1 Cor. 13:9–10). He went on to say in Romans 8:18, "For I consider that the sufferings of this present time are not worthy to be compared with the glory which shall be revealed in us."

This new age will be an elevated state of perfection and harmony beyond that of the garden of Eden. Animals that we now fear, for example, will be amazingly harmless and friendly. Isaiah 11:6–9 says,

> "The wolf also shall dwell with the lamb, the leopard shall lie down with the young goat, the calf and the young lion and the fatling together; and a little child shall lead them. The cow and the bear shall graze; their young ones shall lie down together; and the lion shall

eat straw like the ox. The nursing child shall play by the cobra's hole, and the weaned child shall put his hand in the viper's den. They shall not hurt nor destroy in all My holy mountain, for the earth shall be full of the knowledge of the Lord as the waters cover the sea."

The scientific community may disagree with what this scripture foretells since they often declare certain animals/dinosaurs per their specific makeup, particularly the design of their tusks, as a means of their limitation to being a carnivore or herbivore. God, however, is bigger and greater and is not limited to science. The scripture clearly states that the lion will eat straw.

In fact, God's creation plan did not include animals devouring other animals for food or humankind hunting animals for meat. The creation record states:

And God said, "See, I have given you every herb that yields seed which is on the face of all the earth, and every tree whose fruit yields seed; to you it shall be for food. Also, to every beast of the earth, to every bird of the air, and to everything that creeps on the earth, in which there is life, I have given every green herb for food" (Gen. 1:29–30).

It wasn't until after the great flood of Noah that God told humankind they could now eat meat. (See Genesis 9:1–4).

The scripture indicates all this harmony will take place principally because "the earth shall be filled with the knowledge of the Lord." No doubt even the animals will have a heightened sense of awareness and understanding regarding themselves and the context of their surroundings. God's presence, knowledge, and rulership will have so much effect even on the animal kingdom and the relationship between humankind and animals. Not only that, but where peace has evaded nations and war takes its place, it will be no more. Why? The answer is simply: because the Prince of Peace will be here. "He shall judge between the nations, and rebuke many people; they shall beat their swords into plowshares, and their spears into pruning hooks; nation shall not lift up sword against nation, neither shall they learn war anymore" (Isa. 2:4).

These scripture references obviously do not give the imagery of some utopia in the skies but of actual events and conditions being created, and in some cases recreated, right here on the earth. It is important that we know and understand that while there is in fact a physical heaven where God, His angels, and the saints of old now dwell, God will most certainly bring this heavenly kingdom to the earth. Scripture references such as Isaiah 66:22–24, Zechariah 14, and Revelation 21–22 all show the Lord's recreation, the consummation of all things; His kingship over all the earth; and Him eternally abiding and tangibly dwelling with His creation.

Throughout the ages, speaking about the rapture is often done in a way to challenge and causes one to think, *What if Jesus should come tonight? Would you be ready?* Unfortunately, the more important and pressing question we should really be asking instead, and which is more likely to happen first, is, "What if today is my last day? What if I were to die in an accident on the way home from work, school, etc.? What if I don't wake up from my sleep tonight? What if the doctor said I'm terminally ill and only have three months to live?"

Since tomorrow is not guaranteed to anyone, these questions should become a much more realistic concern and of pressing relevance, rather than sitting back and waiting for any specific sign or context to have a better idea of when Jesus will return. Jesus spoke unto the Pharisees and Sadducees, saying, "When it is evening you say, 'It will be fair weather, for the sky is red'; and in the morning, 'It will be foul weather today, for the sky is red and threatening.' Hypocrites! You know how to discern the face of the sky, but you cannot discern the signs of the times" (Matt. 16:2–3).

Discerning the signs of the times (present day) is far more important than making attempts to fully understand prophetic events of the future. We have today. There is no guarantee we will have tomorrow. Jesus wept over Jerusalem and told them what awaits them because they did not know/embrace the time of their visitation

(Luke 19:41–45). We can't afford to be so caught up in the future that we fail to appreciate God's gift, the present of today. It is what has been given to us, not tomorrow.

If we didn't make the most of the past and make the best decisions, forget about it; yesterday is gone. There is nothing you can do to change the past. The future as well, though it might be promising, is not a guaranteed promise for you and me. It is with this understanding that the scripture issues this warning: "Behold, now is the acceptable time; behold, now is the day of salvation" (2 Cor. 6:2).

To act as if we are masters of our destinies is not only foolish and arrogant but misguided. There is greater wisdom in acknowledging the sovereignty of God, along with the frailness of our humanity, and thus avoid boasting about tomorrow.

James 4:13–15 says,

> "Come now, you who say, "Today or tomorrow we will go to such and such a city, spend a year there, buy and sell, and make a profit"; whereas you do not know what will happen tomorrow. For what is your life? It is even a vapor that appears for a little time and then vanishes away. Instead you ought to say, "If the Lord wills, we shall live and do this or that."

To amplify both the relevance and urgency of now, Jesus said we are to "Store up treasures in heaven where thieves do not break in and steal and where moth do not corrupt. For where your treasure is, there your heart will be also" (Matt. 6:19–21). We are to be consistently living for Jesus and doing service for Him. "For we are His workmanship, created in Christ Jesus for good works, which God prepared beforehand that we should walk in them" (Eph. 2:10).

While we are encouraged to be faithful and consistent servants of Jesus, we are also warned about the consequences of doing such service with the wrong attitude and motive of the heart. Paul says everyone's work will be tried by fire to see what sort it's made of, and some will suffer loss because their work did not endure (1 Cor. 3:11–15).

There used to be a time when pastors were preaching almost nothing but hell, fire, and brimstone! Many people were saved during those days, as people would run to Jesus out of fear of going to hell. Hell was feared, whether or not heaven or Jesus was loved. Given another option other than hell, who would really want to go there? Unfortunately, when someone rejects the grace, mercy, forgiveness, and justifying sacrifice of Jesus Christ through His redemptive work on the cross, they are only left with the justice of God in eternal condemnation.

I would like to break down this section relating to the justice of hell into three sections:

1) God's justice
2) death (spiritual and natural)
3) hell

God's Justice

Found in John 3:16 are indications of both the grace of God and His justice: in the wording, "should not perish but have eternal life." To believe or not to believe works hand in hand as an ultimatum of choice from which forgiveness and reconciliation or condemnation would come. Choosing to believe is to reject unbelief, and choosing unbelief is refusing to believe. Verse 18 says, "He who believes in Him is not condemned; but he who does not believe is condemned *already.*"

Interestingly, the scripture does not put this condemnation as a futuristic situation or event. It says they are "condemned already." What does this mean? It means we were born as condemned sinners and must be saved from this condemnation. It means the unbeliever is guilty as he or she stands. Romans 3:23 says, "For all have sinned and come short of the glory of God." David also said in Psalm 51:5, "Behold, I was brought forth in iniquity, and in sin my mother conceived me."

I remember listing to a sermon from my favorite minister, Adrian Rogers, who in his sermon, titled, "God versus Humanity," said, "Your sins will be pardoned in Christ or punished in hell, but it will never be overlooked." He went on to say, "If God were to let sin go unpunished, He would topple from His throne of holiness."

Ephesians 2:1–3 says,

> "And you He made alive, who were dead in trespass and sins, in which you once walked according to the course of this world, according to the prince of the power of the air, the spirit who now works in the sons of disobedience, among whom also we all once conducted ourselves in the lusts of our flesh, fulfilling the desires of the flesh and of the mind, and *were by nature children of wrath, just as the others.*"

John 3:19 says, "And this is the condemnation, that the light has come into the world, and men loved darkness rather than light, because their deeds were evil." Condemnation does not come because we've sinned and are sinners. In fact, Jesus said He did not come to condemn the world. Condemnation comes, however, because we've rejected God's atonement and forgiveness.

This is the condemnation, the Bible says, that light has come, but men still choose darkness. Had there not been any light, an alternative, then we could cry out to God and say, "This is not right, it's not fair … what happens to mercy? Can You not have mercy and sent us some light? Why are we condemned for all eternity because of someone else's (Adam's) sin?" But what is there to say when God has in fact sent the Light and we not only refuse to believe, but we straight out reject it (Him) because we prefer to remain and "enjoy" the darkness?

Thus, we read in Hebrews 2:1–4:

> "Therefore we must give the more earnest heed to the things we have heard, lest we drift away. For if the word spoken through angels proved steadfast, and every

transgression and disobedience received a just reward, how shall we escape if we neglect so great a salvation, which at the first began to be spoken by the Lord, and was confirmed to us by those who heard Him, God also bearing witness both with signs and wonders, with various miracles, and gifts of the Holy Spirit, according to His own will?"

If we see Jesus only as the loving and forgiving Lamb of God that takes away the sins of the world, our view of Him is incomplete and limited and can cause us to develop misconstrued doctrines. It is imperative that we understand the essential dual role and ministry of our Lord Jesus Christ as both a Lamb and a Lion.

Moses was interested to know the very essence of who God is, and so he asked for God to show him His glory. God responded by telling Moses that no man can see His face and live. But because he had found grace in His sight, God would make an exception, albeit through hiding Moses in the cleft of a rock until He passed by. Then Moses would only see the backside of God, so as to not see God's face and die. Then the Lord passed by and declared to Moses:

"The Lord, the Lord God, merciful and gracious, longsuffering, and abounding in goodness and truth, keeping mercy for thousands, forgiving iniquity and transgression and sin, by no means clearing the guilty" (Ex. 34:6–7).

Psalm 89:14 also says, "Righteousness and justice are the foundation of Your throne; mercy and truth go before Your face." God's justice is based on His righteousness, and His righteousness is also based on His justice. These are not independent of themselves but are unified. His truth and mercy go before Him. In other words, God is more inclined to show/exercise mercy than He is justice. James 2:13 says, "For judgement is without mercy to the one who has shown no mercy. Mercy triumphs over judgement." (See also the book of Jonah).

His truth is also the guiding light by which God exercises His justice and His mercy. Think about it: a child who takes responsibility for his or her wrongdoing, humbly comes forward, and speaks the truth; would that child be more likely to be shown mercy? I would think so. On the other hand, to show mercy to someone who hides the truth and is in fact guilty, it would be counterproductive and be a misplacement of mercy. This is because chances are, the one who's guilty would go free and some innocent person or group would end up being wrongfully convicted and therefore must face justice—which would also be an act of misplaced justice/injustice.

If God were to exercise mercy toward anyone or a group of people we think deserves justice or judgment; and that by God showing mercy He's therefore a God of injustice, this could not be accurately labeled as injustice. The fact is that Jesus took all the punishment and righteous judgement of God upon Himself on our behalf. Someone else (Jesus) paid the price, and that's why we can go free, without paying.

Can God overlook sin? No. In fact, Romans 6:23 says, "For the wages of sin is death, but the gift of God is eternal life." Jesus Christ died for us; He died in our place so we would not have to die for our own sins. We are justified in the sight of God because the ultimate punishment that was ours, Jesus has atoned for, and we are now the benefactors of Christ's death on the cross.

The cross not only represents the unconditional love of God, His mercy, and His grace, but it also represents His justice. Faced with the looming cruelty of the cross in the garden of Gethsemane, Jesus said, "My soul is exceedingly sorrowful, even to death … O My Father, if it is possible, let this *cup* pass from Me; nevertheless, not as I will, but as You will" (Matt. 26:38–39).

A cup is often used in the Bible to symbolize wrath and judgment—the pouring out of it and the drinking of it by whomever the judgement is pronounced. "For thus says the Lord God of Israel, 'Take this cup of fury from My hand, and cause all the nations, to whom I send you, to drink it. And they will drink and stagger and go mad because of the sword that I will send among them'"

(Jer. 25:15–16). "For thus says the Lord, 'Behold, those whose judgement was not to drink of the cup have assuredly drunk. Are you the one who will altogether go unpunished? You shall not go unpunished, but you shall surely drink of it'" (Jer. 49:12).

The extent of God's love and justice is paramount in our preaching of both heaven and hell. It is worthwhile to note that God gave His all—loving us unconditionally, forgiving us, and being willing to forgive us repeatedly, paying our sin debt that He did not owe, all in an effort for us to be reconciled to the Father and have eternal life. He delivered us from condemnation and from His justice apart from grace.

Eternal death and hell, therefore, are the byproduct and subsequent reality of rejecting the gracious gift that God has made readily and easily available to all humankind—for the opposite of believing in Christ and having eternal life is that we will perish. There is no other atonement for sin that God will or can accept, save the one that He provided. So then, God's justice will forbid His grace to be shown to those who reject His grace in the first place. They instead must now face (the Lion of justice) eternal death and an eternity in hell, since they rejected grace and eternal life in the presence of God—heaven.

Death

When Revelation talks about the second death, does anything in particular come to mind? Well, if it says second death, this means there must be a first. Now, there's more to this than what is at the surface. In Genesis, God told Adam and Eve not to touch or to eat from the tree of knowledge of good and evil, because the day in which they do, they would surely die (Gen. 2:16–17). From this standpoint, we understand that death comes in two forms: (1) spiritual death, (2) natural or physical death. Ephesians 2:1–2 says, "And you He made alive, who were dead in trespasses and sins, in which you once walked according to the course of this world."

Adam and Eve died spiritually the moment they disobeyed God.

Their spiritual connection and relationship with God was severed. Isaiah 59:2 says, "Your iniquities have separated you from your God; and your sins have hidden His face from you, so that He will not hear."

To die a natural, physical death is not eternal and is far less severe in the eyes of God than spiritual death and separation from God. We were born into sin and in the condemnation of death. Therefore, Jesus declared that we must be born again, and that unless one is born again, he cannot see the kingdom of God (John 3:3–7). The Bible focuses more on this spiritual state of death (sin) that we were all born into, and the second and final death (damnation and eternal separation from God), than it does regarding physical death.

The book of Hebrews speaks clearly about the reality of living in fear of death (Heb. 2:14–18). But this natural death or dying is temporary and cannot separate us from God. In fact, the apostle Paul indicated that to be absent from the body is to be present with the Lord (2 Cor. 5:1–8). He further declared that nothing (except sin) can separate us from God, saying,

> "Who shall separate us from the love of Christ? Shall tribulation, or distress, or persecution, or famine, or nakedness of peril, or sword? ...For I am persuaded that neither death nor life, nor angels nor principalities nor powers ... nor any other created thing shall be able to separate us from the love of God which is in Christ Jesus our Lord" (Rom. 8:35–39).

Jesus even went as far as declaring that Lazarus was only sleeping, after it was already established that he was dead. This is a perfect example that shows that this physical, natural death, in between the first death and the second death, is not to be feared as much as the second death. Jesus said we shouldn't fear him who can only kill the body, but rather fear Him who can destroy both body and soul in hell (Matt. 10:28).

Fortunately, death is only the doorway that leads into eternity in the intimate, tangible presence of God. It is also the doorway that will lead to an eternity without God, completely void of His presence, for those who choose to live without God. If you choose to live without God, in due time chances are you will be faced to live without Him for all eternity.

It is safe to say there are three forms or stages of death, based on the Bible: (1) spiritual death through sin and relational separation from God—a reality of all humankind through the fall of Adam; (2) physical or natural death—everyone will be faced with the reality of death (except through the rapture) ("It is appointed for men to die once, but after this the judgment" Heb. 9:27); and (3) eternal death/separation from God together with condemnation and everlasting punishment.

Natural or physical death is more common and somewhat understandable to everyone because the living return to the dust, and it is obvious to all. Interestingly enough, the Greek word for death, *thanatos*, refers to both physical and spiritual death.[8] However (special note), in the context of Revelation 20, it is not referring to physical death but of spiritual death ... eternal separation from God!

A few years ago, news broke of three girls who were freed from their captor, Ariel Castro, who had managed to abduct these girls and kept them in captivity for over a decade as he repeatedly raped and abused them. Just about every news channel was airing this news while an entire nation and much of the world was feeling outmost disgust and even hatred toward this man but sincere empathy for the girls.

Not long after Ariel Castro was in custody, he couldn't bear to live in the moment of the spotlight with the shame and possible guilt. He figured it would be best to "end his misery" by taking his own life. This is where so many people get it all wrong. You don't really end your misery by doing something like committing suicide;

---

[8] Zodhiates, Spiros. *The Complete Word Study New Testament: Bringing The Original Text to Life,* (Chattanooga, TN. AMG Publishers, 1991), pg. 919.

you in fact increase the misery by stepping into a state of eternal torment with no possible way of reversing it.

What can be said of the living cannot be said of the dead— namely: "For him who is joined to all the living there is hope, for a living dog is better than a dead lion" (Eccles. 9:4).

Hell

Before I progress too far in addressing this subject matter of hell and the justice of hell, I think it's necessary and important that this foundational truth be quickly established: that this place called hell was created by God as an eternal dwelling place of punishment entirely and strictly for Satan and his angels. According to Matthew 25 Jesus will say of some, as He separates the "sheep from the goats" "depart from Me, you cursed into everlasting fire *prepared for the devil and his angels*" (Matt. 25:41).

In speaking of hell, one thing is certain: those who go there were never given an invitation; they also will have no hope of leaving or of a second chance of God's grace or salvation once they go there. There is simply no way out of hell. (See brief list of scriptures referring to ultimate hell: Matt. 13:41--43; Mark 9:43–44; Rev. 19:20, 20:10, 11–15).

What is also troubling about hell is not just that it's a place; it is also a state of condition and atmosphere. Those who have rejected God will be eternally separated from Him.

There is an unfortunate condition that I call, "The tragedy: when God gives man what they want." There are many who would like nothing to do with God but that God would just leave them alone and give them their space so they can live their lives the way they want. They want to be free from God or anything godly—and God will, unfortunately, grant this request.

Apart from the torment of hell also comes the reality of being totally void of God. He might not be out of mind, but He'll definitely be out of sight, out of reach, and He won't respond to any invitation or plea for mercy whatsoever, no matter how genuine or persistent or the duration of the call. The apostle Paul told the men of Athens,

> "He [God] has made from one blood every nation of men to dwell on all the face of the earth, and has determined their pre-appointed times and the boundaries of their dwellings, so that they should seek the Lord, in the hope that they might grope for Him and find Him, though *He is not far from each one of us*; for in Him we live and move and have our being" (Acts 17:26–28, emphasis added).

Isaiah made it clear that we should not take for granted the privilege we have to reach out to God and for God to respond to us. This scripture ought not to be ignored:

> "Seek the Lord *while He may be found*, call upon Him *while He is near*. Let the wicked forsake his way, the unrighteous man his thoughts; let him return to the Lord, and He will have mercy on him; and to our God, for He will abundantly pardon" (Isa. 55:6–7).

For the sake of those who may not be familiar with the teachings of hell, and for many who may not fully understand this bedrock doctrine within Christianity, please allow me to share one of the most misunderstood scriptures about hell from which also comes misinterpretations. This will also help us to better understand and clarify what the scripture really does teach about hell.

Jesus said,

> "There was a certain rich man, which was clothed in purple and fine linen, and fared sumptuously every day: And there was a certain beggar named Lazarus, which was laid at his gate, full of sores, And desiring to be fed with the crumbs which fell from the rich man's table: moreover the dogs came and licked his sores. And it came to pass, that the beggar died, and was carried by the angels into Abraham's bosom: the rich man also died,

and was buried; And in hell he lift up his eyes, being in torments, and seeth Abraham afar off, and Lazarus in his bosom. And he cried and said, 'Father Abraham, have mercy on me, and send Lazarus, that he may dip the tip of his finger in water, and cool my tongue; for I am tormented in this flame.' But Abraham said, 'Son, remember that thou in thy lifetime receivedst thy good things, and likewise Lazarus evil things: but now he is comforted, and thou art tormented. And beside all this, between us and you there is a great gulf fixed: so that they which would pass from hence to you cannot; neither can they pass to us, that would come from thence.' Then he said, 'I pray thee therefore, father, that thou wouldest send him to my father's house: For I have five brethren; that he may testify unto them, lest they also come into this place of torment.' Abraham saith unto him, 'They have Moses and the prophets; let them hear them.' And he said, 'Nay, father Abraham: but if one went unto them from the dead, they will repent.' And he said unto him, 'If they hear not Moses and the prophets, neither will they be persuaded, though one rose from the dead'" (Luke 16:19–31 KJV).

Some Bible translations use the word *Hades* instead of hell or synonymous with hell. However, in the context of scripture in general and certain wording, the word *hell* certainly does not fit into this context. Not only does hell not fit into this specific context but also of any other suggestion that would indicate someone dying and immediately going straight to hell. Hades is the more appropriate and correct word to describe this introductory transition of life after death.

According to Spiros Zodhiates in the *Word Study Series: The Complete Word Study New Testament*, Hades is defined in the Greek lexical aids as,

"The region of departed spirits of the lost but including departed believers (Luke 16:23). Most probable derivation is from "hado," all-receding. It corresponds to sheol in the Old Testament. Both words have been inadequately translated in the KJV as hell (Ps. 16:10), or the grave (Gen. 37:35), or the pit (Num.16:30, 33). Hades never denotes the physical grave nor is it the permanent region of the lost. Some feel it is the intermediate state between death and the ultimate hell, Gehenna."[9]

Let us examine both this scripture and its meaning in light of other scriptures. This scripture makes it clear that death is not the end of life; it is the entrance to another life. Both men lived two separate lives and thus ended up in two different places. Lazarus was taken to Abraham's bosom, where he was comforted. The rich man was buried but was later seen in Hades, a place in which he was being tormented.

If Hades is the place where all departed spirits go, then it would be fair to conclude that there would be two separate sections in Hades, sort of like a duplex where unit A was a place of torment for the wicked and unbelieving but unit B, or better known as Abraham's bosom, was a place of comfort for the righteous believing saints.

This "duplex" was so uniquely designed that both the wicked and the righteous were able to see and correspond with each other but were forbidden to cross over to the other side.

> "And in hell he lift up his eyes, being in torments, *and seeth Abraham afar off, and Lazarus in his bosom. And he cried and said,* 'Father Abraham, have mercy on me, and send Lazarus, that he may dip the tip of his finger in water, and cool my tongue; for I am tormented in this flame. ...And beside all this, *between us and you there is a great gulf fixed: so that they which would pass from hence to you cannot; neither can they pass to us, that would come from thence'"* (vv. 23–26 KJV).

---

[9]   Zodhiates, Spiros. *The Complete Word Study New Testament: Bringing The Original Text to Life,* (Chattanooga, TN. AMG Publishers, 1991), pg. 881.

This would obviously make sense since any family member seeing another member of their family in torment would definitely want to do something to help. Unfortunately, even the rich man would've turned back the hands of time to redo and relive his life simply to change his eternal fate.

For the rich man, Hades was only like a remand unit in which one is remanded in jail to await trial and/or sentencing. Hades is neither the permanent place for the wicked, nor is Abraham's bosom the permanent place for the righteous. In fact, Jesus, in His death, burial, and resurrection, defeated him who had the power of death (Satan) and took the keys of Hades and death (Rev. 1:18). He also released the saints from Abraham's bosom, ushered them into the very presence of the Lord in heaven, and decommissioned it. If this was not the case, to be absent from the body would never be the equivalent of being present with the Lord (2 Cor. 5:8).

Jesus declared in Revelation 1:18, saying, "I am He who lives, and was dead, and behold, I am alive forevermore. Amen. And I have the keys of Hades and of Death." Jesus is declaring that He alone, and in His own timing, will open the door of Hades and call for the dead that reside there, and they will stand before Him in judgment.

Peter on the day of Pentecost, when he was preaching, made mention of this prophecy in the book of Psalms in relation to Jesus to prove that He was risen from the dead: "For You will not leave my soul in Sheol, nor will You allow Your Holy One to see corruption" (Ps. 16:10).

It's impossible for the rich man or anyone else who have died without accepting God's forgiveness to be in/go to hell since they have not been judged yet. When someone commits a crime or is suspected of committing a crime, there is still the notion of "innocent until proven guilty." Thus, there is a trial, and if one is found guilty, then there comes the judgment of sentencing. The same goes for the heavenly judicial system.

There will be a resurrection not just of the righteous saints but also of the wicked. Revelation 20:11–15 says,

> "Then I saw a great white throne and Him that sat on it, from whose face the earth and the heaven fled away. And there was found no place for them. And I saw the dead, small and great, standing before God, and books were opened. And another book was opened, which is the Book of Life. And the dead were judged according to their works, by the things which were written in the books. The sea gave up the dead which were in it, and Death and Hades delivered up the dead who were in them. And they were judged, each one according to his works. Then Death and Hades were cast into the lake of fire. This is the second death. And anyone not found written in the Book of Life was cast into the lake of fire."

It is worth noting that in this scripture that describes the great judgment of God, even Hades is forced to deliver up the dead who are in it so they can stand before God. It is only then, after this judgment, that unbelievers are cast into eternal fire or hell—Gehenna.

Many people believe hell is not real, let alone eternal. Some believe they're gonna have a "party" in hell. Others believe hell's punishment is not eternal because you are thrown into the lake of fire and are immediately consumed by the flames.

Hell, however, is real and eternal and those who go there do not die physically. Matthew 25:46 says, "And these will go away into *everlasting* punishment, but the righteous into *eternal* life." Everlasting and eternal are synonyms. So eternal life (comfort) is promised to the righteous, while eternal death, the state of spiritual death and separation from God along with torment, is promised to the unrighteous. You cannot punish a dead person. If you beat, kick, cut, etc., a dead person, he or she will feel nothing. It is therefore unconventional to think that God would be punishing the dead for all eternity, who cease to exist or feel anything.

When the unrighteous are raised from the dead in Revelation 20, it would only make sense to conclude that they will somehow possess an "immortal body." How else would they be cast into the lake of fire and not immediately or at all be consumed by the flames? Instead, they are tormented in the flames forever. If God could preserve the three Hebrew boys in the fiery furnace, so much so that they didn't even smell like smoke (see Daniel 3), then He's able to allow anyone to be in the midst of a blazing fire and only to feel the heat and torment of the flames while not being consumed by them.

The rich man said he was being "tormented" in the flames, not consumed by them. This also should stand as an insight into the eternal flames of hell and the eternal, immortal body enduring the flames and its tormenting element.

The word of God speaks for itself:

> "If anyone worships the beast and his image, and receive his mark on his forehead or on his hand, he himself shall also drink of the wine of the wrath of God, which is poured out full strength into the cup of His indignation. He shall be tormented with fire and brimstone in the presence of the holy angels and in the presence of the Lamb. *And the smoke of their torment ascends forever and ever, and they have no rest day or night*, who worship the beast and his image, and whoever receives the mark of his name" (Rev. 14:9–11).

"No rest for the wicked" is more than just a phrase. It will become an unwelcome phase of human history—eternity for those who reject the grace of heaven and are left with the justice of hell. In this regard, we are the masters of our own fate. We are the ones who choose to receive or reject God's forgiveness. He paid a high price to give us eternal life. Why would anyone choose eternal death?

CHAPTER 5

THE ULTIMATE (SECOND) RETURN OF JESUS CHRIST TO RULE AND REIGN

Some may say that there is absolutely nothing restraining the Lord Jesus Christ from returning. This means there are no prophecies that have to be fulfilled or the creation of a certain context in order to usher in the return of Christ. However, careful study of the scripture would indicate otherwise. Jesus cannot and will not return whenever He feels like, because He's given clear prophetic understanding as to when He will return. To do otherwise would prove that God is not a Man of His word.

The prophet Daniel was told that the return of the Ancient of Days would take place when the formation of ten kings (kingdom) rule and/or system is established. Daniel was brought in before King Nebuchadnezzar to interpret the king's dream of a great image of various materials. He noted that a stone was cut out of the mountain without hands that came and smote the image on its feet of iron mixed with clay and broke the entire image to pieces (Dan. 2:31–36).

This image that the king dreamt was a representation of the world empires that would succeed each other from head to toe. The toe section of this image is of primary importance because it is the final part of the image that will parallel the end times.

Since this one prophetic scripture is so important to the study of the end times, as it spans thousands of years in somewhat of a timetable to the consummation of God's plans, it's worth taking a closer look at it together.

King Nebuchadnezzar had a dream he could neither remember nor understand. Thus, he sought for a magician, a soothsayer— anyone who could tell him his dream and its interpretation. Eventually, as Daniel, Hananiah (Shadrach), Mishael (Meshach), and Azariah (Abed-Nego) sought the Lord, the Lord gave them both the dream and its interpretation just as the king was going to kill all the magicians and wise men in his bitter rage, because no one could remind him of his dream or tell him its interpretation.

Daniel begins by saying,

> "You, O king, were watching; and behold, a great image! This great image, whose splendor was excellent, stood before you; and its form was awesome. This image's head was of fine gold, its chest and arms of silver, its belly and thighs of bronze, its legs of iron, its feet partly of iron and partly of clay. You watched while a stone was cut out without hands, which struck the image on its feet of iron and clay, and broke them in pieces. Then the iron, the clay, the bronze, the silver, and the gold were crushed together, and became like chaff from the summer threshing floors; the wind carried them away so that no trace of them was found. And the stone that struck the image became a great mountain and filled the whole earth. This is the dream. Now we will tell the interpretation of it before the king. You, O king, are a king of kings. For the God of heaven has given you a kingdom, power, strength, and glory; and wherever the children of men dwell, or the beast of the field and the birds of the heaven, He has given them into your hand, and has made you ruler over them all—you are this head of gold. But after you shall arise another kingdom inferior to yours; then another, a third kingdom of bronze, which shall rule over all the earth. And the

fourth kingdom shall be as strong as iron, inasmuch as iron breaks in pieces and shatters everything; and like iron that crushes, that kingdom will break in pieces and crush all the others. Whereas you saw the feet and toes, partly of potter's clay and partly of iron, the kingdom shall be divided; yet the strength of the iron shall be in it, just as you saw the iron mixed with ceramic clay. And as the toes of the feet were partly of iron and partly of clay, so the kingdom shall be partly strong and partly fragile. As you saw iron mixed with ceramic clay, they will mingle with the seed of men; but they will not adhere to one another, just as iron does not mix with clay. *And in the days of these kings the God of heaven will set up a kingdom which shall never be destroyed* ... Inasmuch as you saw that the stone was cut out of the mountain without hands and that it broke in pieces the iron, the bronze, the clay, the silver, and the gold—the great God has made known to the king what will come to pass after this. The dream is certain, and the interpretation is sure" (Dan. 2:31–46).

Not only is this scripture of great significance in end-time prophecy, but its unfolding accuracy, even from a secular standpoint, is also beyond dispute. This was a unique prophetic timetable that the Lord had revealed through the discourse of King Nebuchadnezzar and Daniel; but the Lord also confirms and affirms this directly to Daniel in chapters 7 and 8 from a perspective that Daniel, a Jew, would be more familiar with. Since Daniel was familiar with animals, especially through the sacrificial system, God used animals to represent the same world empires that He had previously showed the pagan king Nebuchadnezzar, who was more accustomed to materials like gold, silver, bronze, etc.

Anyone can do a careful search through history and would no doubt come to the same conclusion—that the events of the Bible as it deals with these world empires are as accurate as the Bible foretold— namely: that the Persian empire would conquer the Babylonian empire, the Grecian empire, conquering the Persian empire (under

Alexander the great), and the Roman empire conquering the Grecian empire and much of the known world.

Rome was symbolic of the iron that breaks in pieces, and also the nondescript beast of Daniel 7:7–24. This beast (kingdom) was so terrifying and different than all the rest that it terrified Daniel and left him somewhat disoriented and confused. It was also declared to Daniel that from within this beast (kingdom) would arise ten horns (kings) and that yet another horn (king) would arise from the ten, who would be different from all previous ones.

Many pundits of end-time prophecy were amazed at the formation of the euro zone, the European Union. Many believe that the reuniting of Europe is nothing short of the rebirth of the old Roman Empire under the disguise of a new world power, but obviously with much less influence, dominance, and cohesiveness as represented in the dysfunctionality of having iron mixed with clay.

Regardless of what this all means, what or who these kings or kingdoms represents, the scripture is clear, that it is within this context that the God of heaven will come as the symbolic stone cut out of the mountain and destroy the image—the representation of human rule and government.

This great image of Nebuchadnezzar's dream along with the seventy weeks of Daniel 9 are the two main timetables God has set/established in dealing with human history and the events surrounding the last days. If one seeks to gain a better understanding of the end times, then studying these two prophetic revelations is extremely important. It will be of great encouragement when studying the image and looking back at history to find out that all has been fulfilled except the formation of the "ten toes." The seventy weeks will be just as encouraging, as we will clearly see that only the final week (seven years) is yet to be fulfilled. The bottom line is, both timetables are running parallel and are climaxing to their final prophetic fulfillment.

As I've mentioned before, attempting to teach end-time prophecy requires an in-depth use and look at scriptures, because our questions mainly arise from the verses we read, and more often than not, the answers we need are also found within those scriptures.

One must also be careful in what one accepts as true scripture—free from all personal and manipulative interpretations and teaching. I remember, for example, hearing of a teaching that was "revealing" what the seven thunders uttered in Revelation 10 meant. John, however, was forbidden by the angel to write the things the seven thunders uttered. Since John was forbidden to write what he saw and heard, who was or who is the privileged one to write it, and where in the Bible is such revelation revealed within the context of scripture? Such teaching is unfounded and should simply be rejected.

Now, having said all that, I believe that scripture clearly paints this second return of Christ distinct from His return in the rapture of 1 Thessalonians 4 and 1 Corinthians 15. I do not believe we can unite these two scriptures with Revelation 19. The account of Jesus' return in Revelation 19 states:

> "Now I saw heaven opened, and behold, a white horse. And He who sat on him was called Faithful and True, and in righteousness He judges and makes war. His eyes were like a flame of fire, and on His head were many crowns. He had a name written that no one knew except Himself. He was clothed with a robe dipped in blood, and His name is called The Word of God. And the armies in heaven, clothed in fine linen, white and clean, followed Him on white horses. Now out of His mouth goes a sharp sword, that with it He should strike the nations. And He Himself treads the winepress of the fierceness and wrath of Almighty God. And He has on His robe and on His thigh a name written: KING OF KINGS AND LORD OF LORDS ... And I saw the beast, the kings of the earth, and their armies, gathered together to make war against Him who sat on the horse and against His army. Then the beast was captured, and with him the false prophet who worked signs in his

presence, by which he deceived those who received the mark of the best and those who worshiped his image" (vv. 11–21).

The picture of Jesus' return in 1 Thessalonians 4, coming to meet His Church as the saints are caught up to meet Him in the air, is of profound contrast to an angry God with fire in His eyes and His robe dipped in blood, coming to make war and to conquer. This is not a picture of a bridegroom coming to meet His bride. Here again Mr. Hank Hanegraaff clearly does not believe in the rapture, or from what I understand from his writings, a physical heaven.

Mr. Hanegraaff states:

> "As bible scholars have duly noted, Paul's teaching in 1 Thessalonians 4 runs directly parallel to his teachings in 1 Corinthians 15. Together they represent the blessed hope that at Christ's coming the end will come … Nowhere does the text say that when Christ comes down from heaven "with a loud command, with the voice of an archangel and with the trumpet call of God" (1 Thessalonians 4:16) that Christ will hover with us in midair, suddenly change directions, and escort us to mansions in heaven."[10]

While I agree with Mr. Hanegraaff that the scripture does not clearly indicate Christ returning back to heaven with His resurrected saints, it also does not clearly show Christ coming and making landfall on the earth as Revelation 19 indicates, and in consort with Zechariah 14. Neither does it say the resurrected saints who go up to meet the Lord in the air turn around to come back down to the earth. That would be pointless. Why resurrect and have the saints caught up in the clouds only to have them return immediately?

---

[10] Hanegraaff, Hank. *The Apocalypse Code: Find Out What The Bible Really Says About The End Times And Why it Matters Today.* (Nashville, TN. Thomas Nelson. 2007), Pg. 58.

Zechariah 14:1–14 puts the ultimate return of Jesus Christ to earth this way:

> "Behold, the day of the Lord is coming, and your spoil will be divided in your midst. For I will gather all the nations to battle against Jerusalem; the city shall be taken, the houses rifled, and the women ravished. Half the city shall go into captivity, but the remnant of the people shall not be cut off from the city. Then the Lord will go forth and fight against those nations, as He fights in the day of battle. *And in that day His feet will stand on the mount of Olives, which faces Jerusalem on the east.* And the Mount of Olives shall be split in two, from east to west, making a very large valley; half of the mountain shall move toward the north and half of it toward the south ... *Thus the Lord God will come, and all the saints with You.* It shall come to pass in that day that there will be no light; the lights will diminish. It shall be one day which is known to the Lord—neither day nor night. But at evening time it shall happen that it will be light. And in that day it shall be that living waters shall flow from Jerusalem, half of them toward the eastern sea and half of them toward the western sea; in both summer and winter it shall occur. And the Lord shall be King over all the earth ... All the land shall be turned into a plain from Geba to Rimmon south of Jerusalem ... The people shall dwell in it; and no longer shall there be utter destruction, but Jerusalem shall be safely inhabited. And this shall be the plague with which the Lord will strike all the people who fought against Jerusalem: their flesh shall dissolve while they stand on their feet, their eyes shall dissolve in their sockets, and their tongues shall dissolve in their mouths. It shall come to pass in that day that a great panic from the Lord will be among them. Everyone will seize the hand of his neighbor, and raise his hand against his neighbor's hand; Judah also will fight at Jerusalem. And the wealth of all the

> surrounding nations shall be gathered together: gold,
> silver, and apparel in great abundance"

This is not a picture of the rapture; this is the ultimate second coming of Jesus Christ to "tread the winepress of the fierceness and wrath of Almighty God" (Rev. 19:15). He is coming to rule and to reign as the eternal King of kings and Lord of lords. Every manmade authority and government will be subdued under His lordship.

Enoch prophesied, "Behold, the Lord comes with ten thousands of His saints, to execute judgment on all, to convict all who are ungodly among them of all their ungodly deeds which they have committed in an ungodly way, and of all the harsh things which ungodly sinners have spoken against Him" (Jude 14). The apostle Paul's teaching of 1 Thessalonians 4 and 1 Corinthians 15 does not correlate to this dreadful appearance of Jesus Christ. In fact, the context of 1 Corinthians 15 is that of the resurrection—being resurrected with a glorified body as we are changed from mortal to immortality; not of God coming to make war.

It is impossible for me to study the scriptures and conclude these two main events of Christ's return to be one and the same event. But rather, each of Christ's comings to earth are all unique and distinct in their own way, function, and purpose. Here is a sample breakdown of Christ's coming to earth:

- Christ's first coming: God sending His Son to die for us; the virgin birth of the Messiah. Supporting scriptures: Gen. 3:15; Deut. 18:15, 16; Ps. 2:1–9; 22:1–18; Isa. 7:14; 9:6–7; 11:1–5; 53:1–12; Dan. 9:26; Mic. 5:2.
- Christ's "intermediate" return/the rapture: Christ's return for the saints, His sealed possession, to deliver us from His impending wrath. Supporting scriptures: John 14:1-4; 1 Cor. 15:12–58; 1 Thess. 4:13–18; 5:1–11.
- Christ's Second (ultimate) coming: Jesus returns to rule and reign and to judge the world in righteousness. Supporting

scriptures: Dan. 7:13, 14; Zech. 14:1–21; Matt. 24:29–31; 25:31–46; Rev. 19:11–21.

I recall back in 1999, just before the year 2000, how there was worldwide pandemonium about Y2K and possibly the end of the world. The year 2012 saw a similar degree of chaos as people referred to the Mayan calendar, which supposedly would end December 21, 2012. People's fear brought enormous profit to various businesses, included the Hollywood movie *2012*. There were also other predictions of the end of the world, such as May 21, 2011. Regarding all these predictions, countless Christians were sucked up in the fear of the moment along with unbelievers.

Many sold their homes, cashed in their life savings, quit their jobs, and so on, all in an effort to support "prophets" like Harold Camping and his apocalyptic prediction of the rapture and the end of the world. What was so troubling about all this was how quickly and easily people bought into these self-claimed prophets and their predictions. It was as if people turned off all basic reasoning and rational thinking. If the world was coming to an end, why are you asking for my money? Why should I sell my house, among other things, to support you? If you the prophet believe so strongly in what you're preaching, then you should be the first to sell your house, quit your job, and start evangelizing the streets. When people are fearful, they will buy into anything and unfortunately sell everything.

However, if we truly believe the word of God as we Christians say we do, then no one should've budged regarding these erroneous predictions about the rapture or the end of the world. Simply put, there are countless end-time prophecies that have not yet been fulfilled. Thus, it would be impossible for the end of the world to be upon us without these events first coming to pass. If that weren't the case, God would be the biggest liar of all time. Not only that, but it would clearly demonstrate that He is not in control and that He was wrong about a lot of things; and ultimately His word cannot be trusted.

Consider, for example: has the battle of Armageddon taken place yet? Has the mark of the beast (666) been implemented already? Has the Antichrist stepped into his predestined role with a peace deal in the Middle East? Have the two witnesses of Revelation 11 appeared and fulfilled their prophesied purpose? The list of end-time prophetic questions yet to be fulfilled goes on and on.

So why do we fall for false doctrine so easily? It is sad because it shows how easily some can be deceived. Any prophet, pastor, teacher, whomever they may be, who declares to you a date for the rapture should be "red flagged." Reject any such teaching! These teachings are so flawed that they don't even have a basis. Contextually speaking, as I've indicated before, if someone were to find him or herself within the final week (seven years) of Daniel's seventy weeks prophecy, then yes, there can be a reasonable estimate as to when Christ will return. But outside of that biblical context, we have no context.

We need not hunker down in expensive bunkers in an attempt to outlast the tribulation. For one, we shouldn't plan on being here. Two, there will be no escaping the tribulation. As 2012 drew near, I can remember saying to some Christian brethren, "Why are you panicking? Why are you overcome with fear like the rest of the world?" If we believe God's word is true, and that He's faithful to His word, then we should trust Him, and stand on His word. "These words are faithful and true. 'And the Lord God of the holy prophets sent His angel to show His servants the things which must shortly take place. Behold, I am coming quickly! Blessed is he who keeps the words of the prophecy of this book'" (Rev. 22:6–7).

When I was in Bible college and studying end-time prophecy, one thing I remember being clearly emphasized by my teachers was, "Context, context, context." That is the key when studying the scriptures. Giving attention to things like culture, grammar, and even geography can also play an important part in the exegesis of God's word.

Hanegraaff for his part clearly does a disservice to the scriptures by confining them to his limited interpretation and not within its broader context. Permit me to share a portion of Hanegraaff's disposition on the abomination of desolation, followed by my discourse:

> "As Jesus was addressing a first-century audience when he spoke of the destruction of the temple, so too he was addressing his contemporaries when he said, "So when you see standing in the holy place 'the abomination that causes desolation,' spoken of by the prophet Daniel— let the reader understand—then let those who are in Judea flee to the mountains ..." (Matthew 24:15–21). The abomination of desolation spoken of by Jesus, had been prophesied six centuries earlier by Daniel, who wrote, "His armed forces will rise up to desecrate the temple fortress and will abolish the daily sacrifice. Then they will set up the abomination that causes desolation. With flattery he will corrupt those who have violated the covenant, but the people who know their God will firmly resist him" (Daniel 11:31–32). In 167 BC Daniel's prophecy became an unforgettable reality when Antiochus IV Epiphanes took Jerusalem by force, abolished temple sacrifices, erected an abominable altar to Zeus Olympus, and violated the Jewish covenant by outlawing the Sabbath observance. Therefore, when Jesus referenced the desolation spoken of the prophet Daniel, everyone in his audience knew precisely what he was talking about. The annual Hanukkah celebration ensured that they would ever remember the Syrian antichrist who desecrated the temple fortress... Had God not supernaturally intervened through the agency of Judas Maccabaeus, the epicenter of their theological and sociological identity would have been destroyed, not just desecrated."[11]

---

[11] Hanegraaff, Hank. *The Apocalypse Code, Find Out What The Bible Really Says About The End Times And Why it Matters Today.* (Nashville, TN. Thomas Nelson. 2007), Pg. 87, 88.

This position and understanding taken by Hanegraaff is absolutely flawed. Yes, Jesus was using the prophecy of Daniel and the desecration of the temple by Antiochus IV Epiphanes to highlight a prophetic reality among His audience. But to limit it solely to that historical occurrence is neither sufficient nor accurate. Jesus was no doubt declaring a twofold prophecy—part of which was already a well-known historical fact, and the other still yet to come.

There was yet a futuristic prophecy in the utterance of Jesus. In fact, the context of Daniel's prophecy does not find contextual and ultimate fulfillment in the historical event of Antiochus IV Epiphanes. Daniel 9:27 says, "Then he shall confirm a covenant with many for one week; *but in the middle of the week he shall bring an end to sacrifice and offering.* And on the wing of *abomination shall be one who makes desolate*, even until the consummation, which is determined, is poured out on the desolate."

Even if there were some form of agreement between the nation of Israel and the Syrians (Antiochus IV Epiphanes), it is unlikely that it was a time-sensitive agreement and precisely timed or coincidentally broken in the middle of a seven-year time frame. This was not the case historically.

Where we do find contextual and ultimate fulfillment of both Daniel's and Jesus' prophecy, however, is in the last days—leading up to the ultimate return of Jesus. Permit me to highlight 2 Thessalonians 2:1–10 once more:

> "Now, brethren, concerning the coming of our Lord Jesus Christ and our gathering together to Him, we ask you, not to be soon shaken in mind or troubled, either by spirit or by word or by letter, as if from us, as though the day of Christ had come. Let no one deceive you by any means; for that Day will not come unless the falling away comes first, and the man of sin is revealed, the son of perdition, who opposes and *exalts himself above all that is called God or that is worshiped, so that he sits as God in the temple of God, showing himself that he is God.* Do you not remember that when I was still with you I told you

these things? And now you know what is restraining, that *he may be revealed in his own time.* For the mystery of lawlessness is already at work; only He who now restrains will do so until He is taken out of the way. And then the lawless one will be revealed, *whom the Lord will consume with the breath of His mouth and destroy with the brightness of His coming.* The coming of the lawless one is according to the working of Satan, with all power, signs, and lying wonders, and with all unrighteous deception among those who perish, because they did not receive the love of the truth, that they might be saved."

This scripture is pretty clear that there is yet to be a future "abomination of desolation" in the nation of Israel, within a rebuilt temple. It's not rocket science to understand and conclude that Paul is speaking not from a historical viewpoint but a futuristic one. It certainly was not the coming of Jesus Christ that destroyed Antiochus IV Epiphanes.

Second Thessalonians 2:1–10 coincides with First Thessalonians 5:1–3, which says,

"But concerning the times and the seasons, brethren, you have no need that I should write to you. For you yourselves know perfectly that the Day of the Lord so comes as a thief in the night. For *when they say, "Peace and safety!" then sudden destruction comes upon them as labor pains upon a pregnant woman.* And they shall not escape."

The apostle Paul ties in "peace and safety" with "sudden destruction." He made reference to when, "They say peace and safety." The "they" he's referring to is no doubt his fellow Jewish brethren (2:14–16), of whom Daniel's one-week (seven-year) covenant period that will be broken at the midpoint is referring to. Furthermore, Paul said the man of sin who sets up/causes the abomination of desolation will be destroyed by the Lord Jesus Christ Himself at His ultimate return.

In our attempted exegesis of scriptures, especially relating to end-time prophecy, we should do so with grace and humility. Far be it from any of us whether self-proclaimed or widely accepted scholars, or even just an average student of the scriptures and of prophecy, that we would promote and defend our understanding and interpretation of eschatology as completely God inspired and free from the slightest error. We may disagree on many different points, and that's okay. What is of greater importance and should be the bottom line is that we believe and uphold the foundational principles of the word of God and of salvation. Whether or not we understand eschatology, it is not grievously detrimental to our Christian walk.

In reading Hanegraaff's book *The Apocalypse Code*, after a while it became more and more difficult as it started to put a bitter taste in my mouth. Almost from start to finish, Hanegraaff set out on an embarrassing and belittling discourse of disrespect and disproving of Tim LaHaye, the author of the well-known *Left Behind* series. Tim LaHaye was not and is not teaching heresy that threatens the believer's eternal security. If that were the case, then yes, his teachings should be outright confronted, rejected, and clarified. But in fact, much of the Church's understanding of end-time events is in unison with LaHaye's.

Notwithstanding, whenever in any way we attempt to have full knowledge and revelation of all Scripture, that's when we're more in danger of erring and leading others astray. Nothing is wrong with saying, "I'm not too sure about that one; give me some time to study it a little more." Furthermore, some insights into prophecy will not be fully revealed until we draw even closer to the end. It's not because we are smarter than previous generations why we are now understanding many of the prophetic mysteries of the last days; it's because the words were shut up and the book "sealed until the time of the end" (Dan. 12:4). We are the privileged generation to whom all these revelations are now being given.

The Holy Spirit is the only "Bible answer Spirit," who is completely infallible in all His discourse and insights; not the "Bible answer man" Mr. Hanegraaff. We try our best by the leading of the

Holy Spirit to dissect the word of God, to study to show ourselves approved, a workman not needed be ashamed, but one who rightly divides the word of truth (2 Tim. 2:15). The truth is, we are subject to misinterpretation. Therefore, we should always be gracious and graceful, not arrogant or dogmatic.

Developing a habit like that of the Bereans, who according to Acts 17:10–13, after the word was preached to them, went and searched the scriptures to find out whether those things were true or not. This is a healthy habit and principle to foster in our exploration of the scriptures. This is in part why I've been sharing so many scriptures for you, the reader, to see for yourselves and in an effort to save you the time of researching while you read. But regardless, believers should always be encouraged to read, search, and study the scriptures for themselves, while asking the Holy Spirit to open their eyes and hearts to revelatory truth of His word.

Whether our position is pre-trib, mid-trib, or post-trib, we can and should all agree that Jesus Christ is coming again! If we are living for Him and keeping our robes clean, then the timing of His coming is almost irrelevant. In fact, many of us may even die before the Lord puts in His appearance. The most urgent and pressing reality of our questions should be: are we ready to meet Him— whether He comes to meet us or we go to meet Him through death?

Jesus' final appearance and message to His disciples and followers was on the Mount of Olives, where He told them to wait for the promise of the Father, the Holy Spirit.

> "Now when He had spoken these things, while they watched, He was taken up, and a cloud received Him out of their sight. And two men stood by them in white apparel, who also said, "Men of Galilee, why do you stand gazing up into heaven? This same Jesus, who was taken up from you into heaven, will so come in like manner as you saw Him go into heaven" (Acts 1:9–11).

Unfortunately, Hanegraaff goes as far as dismissing much of the prophetic language as either similes, metaphors, etc., as if nothing in the imagery of the end times should be taken literal. For example, he says,

> "Like the old testament prophets, Jesus employs the symbolism of clouds to warn his hearers that as judgment fell on Egypt, so too, judgment would soon befall Jerusalem. Using final consummation language to characterize a near-future event, the Master of Metaphor declares, 'At that time the sign of the Son of Man will appear in the sky, all the nations of the earth will mourn. They will see the Son of Man coming on the clouds of the sky, with power and great glory'" (Mathew 24:30).[12]

Why is it unthinkable or unlikely that Jesus will return literally on clouds? As mentioned in Acts 1:9–11, Jesus went up into a cloud into heaven, and the disciples were told He would return in like manner. There is no reason to not take this scripture at face value. We need not try to be sophisticated and complicate the word of God. The Bible also said God descended on Mount Sinai in a thick cloud (Ex. 34:5). (See also Exodus 19:9, 16 and Numbers 11:25, 12:5.)

Revelation 1:7–8 further declares,

> "Behold, He is coming with clouds, and every eye will see Him, even they who pierced Him. And all the tribes of the earth will mourn because of Him. Even so, Amen. "I am the Alpha and the Omega, the Beginning and the End," says the Lord, who is and who was and who is to come, the Almighty."

Jesus (God) came to earth in the humble form of a man and metaphorically as the "Lamb of God" to atone for the sins of this world. However, the Bible also declares that He is coming back!

---

[12] Hanegraaff, Hank. *The Apocalypse Code: Find Out What The Bible Really Says About The End Times And Why it Matters Today.* (Nashville, TN. Thomas Nelson. 2007), pg. 26.

His ultimate return will not be to preach and heal or in any sort of ministry to which He was engaged in while on earth the first time around. This time He's coming as judge; He's coming not as a peaceful or sacrificial Lamb but as a conquering Lion!

He's coming to receive His purchased possession—all those who have been bought by His precious blood (1 Corinthians 6:19–20). He will also execute righteous judgment on those who rejected His salvation (John 3:18–19).

It is without question that we are living in the last days as we're witnessing one of the greatest fulfillments of end-time Bible prophecy: the nation of Israel. Not only is Israel of paramount significance in the unfolding of the last days, but it also stands as a testament to the God of the Bible who has been involved in the dealings of nations throughout history. And thus, Israel stands as another tangible piece of evidence to the faithfulness of God and His promises.

Among the figurative languages used of Israel, the fig tree is of unique interest when studying the last days. Of the many scriptures identifying Israel as the fig tree, Hosea 9:10; Judges 9:11; Jeremiah 8:13; 24:1–10, Joel 1:6–7, to list a few, Jeremiah 24:1–10 is of great significance and application and is worth quoting:

> "The Lord showed me, and there were two baskets of figs set before the temple of the Lord, after Nebuchadnezzar king of Babylon had carried away captive Jeconiah the son of Jehoiakim, king of Judah, and the princes of Judah ... Then the Lord said to me, 'What do you see, Jeremiah?' And I said, 'Figs, the good figs, very good; and the bad, very bad, which cannot be eaten, they are so bad.' Again the word of the Lord came to me, saying, "Thus says the Lord, the God of Israel: like these good figs, so will I acknowledge those who are carried away captive from Judah, whom I have sent out of this place for their own good, into the land of the Chaldeans. For I will set My eyes on them for good, and I will bring them back

to this land; I will build them and not pull them down, and I will plant them and not pluck them up" (vv. 1–6).

The Lord speaks of Israel (the fig tree) on whom He has set His eyes to do them good, even though they are carried away captive to Babylon, that He will see to it they return. Though throughout biblical times they have on at least two main occasions experienced exile and return, there was yet to be a final exile and return of the Jewish people from all the nations back to their ancestral homeland. Regarding this final exile, Jesus said, "And they will fall by the edge of the sword, and be led away captive into all nations. And Jerusalem will be trampled by Gentiles until the times of the Gentiles are fulfilled" (Luke 21:24).

With the destruction of Jerusalem in AD 70 by the Romans, the Jews were dispersed throughout the world, fulfilling this prophecy of Jesus. They have seen much hatred and attempts to exterminate them, and the Holocaust is a stark reminder of this reality. But when it was all said and done, after WWII on May 14, 1948, the United Nations declared Israel a sovereign nation state with the land of Israel as their geographical borders. The coming together of these events were also prophesied in Isaiah 66:8, which states: "Who has heard such a thing? Who has seen such a thing? Shall the earth be made to give birth in one day? Or shall a nation be born at once? For as soon as Zion was in labor, she gave birth to her children."

What the United Nations did on May 14, 1948, was not the birth of a nation, but rather its rebirth—the beginning of the fig tree budding and coming back to life. And from this context, we see numerous scriptures of God gathering His people back to their homeland. Not only are Jews flocking back to Israel (Aliyah—Jewish migration) from all over the world and flourishing as the figurative fig tree, but so are the literal fig tress themselves, because the land has a unique connection to the people and the people to the land. Here is a brief list of some of the scriptures that foretold God's plan to bring back the Jews to their native land: Isaiah 43:5–7;

Jeremiah 30:18–22; 31:7–10; Ezekiel 36:6–11, 24; 37:1–14, 21–22; 38:1–9; Hosea 3:4–5.

Of these scriptures listed, I think it's worthwhile to share Jeremiah 31:7–10:

> "For thus says the Lord: 'Sing with gladness for Jacob, and shout among the chief of the nations; proclaim, give praise, and say, 'O Lord, save Your people, the remnant of Israel!' Behold, I will bring them from the north country, and gather them from the ends of the earth, among them the blind and the lame, the woman with child and the one who labors with child, together; a great throng shall return there. They shall come with weeping, and with supplications I will lead them ... *For I am a Father to Israel*, and Ephraim is My firstborn. Hear the word of the Lord, O nations, and declare it in the isles afar off, and say, 'He who scatters Israel will gather him, and keep him as a shepherd does his flock.'"

Israel did not steal Palestinians' land, nor are they occupying land that is not theirs. This is the land of the Bible, Bethlehem, Samaria, Judea, Jerusalem—areas that were all settled by Jews and played important roles in our biblical text. There are those who would like to rewrite history in regard to this issue of land ownership. But any attempt to do so will fail, because what has been written has been written—written on the pages of ancient texts and on the hearts of those who know the truth. The ancient connection of the Jews to the land of Israel cannot be denied. And let us not forget, the Bible is among one of the greatest, oldest, and most accurate historical books. It's about time the United Nations comes to the realization that they cannot overrule God!

Joel 2 also makes it clear that God is opposed to any and every attempt to divide the land of Israel, and it also shows why Israel is one of the most if not the single most significant end-time prophecy on which numerous other prophecies hinges, because Israel's regathering sets in motion (context) the unfolding of the rest. Up until Israel was again in possession of the land of Israel, countless prophecies were at a standstill:

> "For behold, in those days and at that time, *when I bring back the captives of Judah and Jerusalem, I will also* gather all nations, and bring them down to the Valley of Jehoshaphat; and I will enter into judgment with them there on account of My people, My heritage Israel, whom they have scattered among the nations; they have also divided up My land" (vv. 1–2).

It's one of the smallest nations in the Middle East, yet Israel keeps dominating the news for multiple reasons, but most notably because they are and will be the focal point as a nation in the last days. The prophetic scriptures are being played out right in front of our very eyes. Nations are plotting the destruction of the state of Israel in secret and openly. The nation of Iran, for example, has made known time and time again their desire to wipe Israel off the map. Psalm 83 has long foretold this time:

> "Do not keep silent, O God! Do not hold Your peace, and do not be still, O God! For behold, Your enemies make a tumult; and those who hate You have lifted up their head. They have taken crafty counsel against Your people, and consulted together against Your sheltered ones. They have said, "Come, and let us cut them off from being a nation, that the name of Israel may be remembered no more." For they have consulted together with one consent; they form a confederacy against You" (vv. 1–5).

All such attempts to destroy Israel will fail, as they did when several Arab nations attacked them at their rebirth and regathering of 1948, the Yom Kippur War, the Six-Day War, the future war of Psalm 83, Ezekiel 38 and 39, and Armageddon. Israel will continue to dominate international and Middle East headlines for the remaining future because they are central to the last days.

Jesus said that when you see the fig tree budding, then we will see and know that summer is near and that the generation that lives to see this event, among other things, will not pass away till all things are fulfilled (Luke 21:20–33). By drawing attention to the fig tree, Jesus was saying that Israel will be a clear prophetic clock to watch in the last days and that the generation that witnesses Israel's rebirth would undoubtedly be the last generation.

If the generation that saw the rebirth of Israel in 1948 is the last generation, then it means our generation is the generation in which all remaining prophecies will be fulfilled. It is therefore then reasonable to ask, "How long is a generation?" There isn't a clear consensus among Bible teachers as to how long the Bible defines a generation to be. But I will briefly highlight three often-referred-to understandings of a generation and share where I stand.

Some view a generation to be forty years. The understanding for this view comes from the wandering in the wilderness for forty years because the people rebelled against the Lord. For the forty days that the spies went to spy out the land, God made each day equivalent to one year in the desert. "So the Lord's anger was aroused against Israel, and He made them wander in the wilderness forty years, until all the generation that had done evil in the sight of the Lord was gone" (Num. 32:13). However, if we look carefully at the story, we'll see that it was only those who were twenty years and older who died in the wilderness. But those who were two, five, ten years old, etc., were also witnesses of the mighty works of God, while others were born in the wilderness. These would all be considered part of that generation as well. (See the full story in Numbers 13–14).

The second view of a generation comes from Psalm 90:9–10, which says, "For all our days have passed away in Your wrath; we finish our years like a sigh. The days of our lives are seventy years; and if by reason of strength they are eighty years, yet their boast is only labor and sorrow; for it is soon cut off, and we fly away." Between those who were born in the wilderness, being one year old, until those who were twenty years and older all died, the one-year-old would then be forty to forty-one years old, while the nineteen-year-old would be fifty-nine or sixty. So again, these two generation timelines are fairly close.

However, the third view indicates the possibility of a generation being one hundred years. In Genesis 15:13–16 the Lord spoke to Abram and said,

> "Know certainly that your descendants will be strangers in a land that is not theirs, and will serve them, and they will afflict them *four hundred years*. And also the nation whom they serve I will judge; afterward they shall come out with great possessions. Now as for you, you shall go to your fathers in peace; you shall be buried at a good old age. *But in the fourth generation they shall return here.*"

In this text, God clearly unites the four hundred years as being synonymous to four generations, which is to say one hundred years is for one generation.

Of the three views, my position is with the latter, 100 years being the longest allotment for a generation. However, some will go as far as saying a generation can potentially be 120 years. This view is based on Genesis 6:3, where God said His Spirit will not always strive with man because he is flesh, and that his days would only be 120 years. Seventy years from the rebirth of Israel brings us to 2018; 100 years brings us to 2048; and to the very extreme, 120 years brings us to 2068.

The reason why I do not focus on the 120-year timeline is because scripture later revealed that God had once more decreased the number of years allotted to man's life to approximately 70 to 80 years.

Regardless of our views of the length of a generation, I believe it is fair to limit it between 40 and 120 years. As we approach the year 2018, it is evident that the applicable generational time line is not 40 years or 70 years since there are still unique prophecies to be fulfilled. It can only therefore be 100 years or 120 years. My personal view, as I've mentioned, is to embrace the generation of

100 years, primarily because of how the Lord used it in the text of Genesis 15, and the fact that the 70-year timeline can no longer be feasible, considering 2018 is already upon us. Also, within any given generation or timeline, we would still need to account for a 7-year peace deal.

These generational timelines however, should only be viewed as an enormous general context to which there are no indications that it will be fully utilized or maximized. In terms of a hundred-year generation approach to whom the prophecy would apply, that it would not pass away until all things are fulfilled, it may take eighty, ninety, or even ninety-five years for all things to come to pass. Therefore, in the broader context of Israel being reborn and the generation that witnessed this event, we will find even greater, more specific signs (context) that will indicate the return of Jesus Christ, a near and present reality.

As we look at our world today, our hearts are stricken with grief, anger, and frustration at the evil, the violence, the wars, the corruption, the starvation, and on and on, that paints an almost-hopeless picture for humankind. We are forced to ask the question: "If there is a God, where are You? How could a loving God allow all this evil to go on? Some who believe in God may even want to start doubting the validity of His word and promises. Or they may simply conclude that God is not in control.

While it is true that Satan is the god of this world (2 Cor. 4:4), this is by no means suggesting that God is not sovereign. Just as in the case of Job, God allows Satan a degree of freedom to do his evil biddings. Notwithstanding, all of earth's problems cannot be blamed on the devil. We as humans have been acting out of greed, selfishness, corruption, control, self-indulgence, and all such things that in more ways than one help to facilitate much evil and pain on the earth.

Thus, we look not just for a heavenly city whose builder and marker is God (Hebrews 11:9–10); but we also look forward to the ultimate return of Jesus Christ and the consummation and regeneration of all things.

We are encouraged by the reassuring words in Revelation 21:1–5, which says,

> "Now I saw a new heaven and a new earth, for the first heaven and the first earth had passed away. Also there was no more sea. Then I, John, saw the holy city, New Jerusalem, coming down out of heaven from God, prepared as a bride adorned for her husband. And I heard a loud voice from heaven saying, "Behold, the tabernacle of God is with men, and He will dwell with them, and they shall be His people. God Himself will be with them and be their God. And God will wipe away every tear from their eyes; there shall be no more death, nor sorrow, nor crying. There shall be no more pain, for the former things have passed away." Then He who sat on the throne said, "Behold, I make all things new." And He said to me, "Write, for these words are true and faithful."

Hallelujah! All hope is not lost for humankind. It's a comforting reassurance in the midst of a world full of evil and violence that God will soon rid this world of all evil, including the force and creature that instigates much of it, the devil himself.

Our death may easily precede the return of Jesus Christ. Ultimately whether we can know the timing or context of His return, or don't even care to know, this will be a certain prophetic event in the future. This is a fundamental truth and promise of the Bible.

The apostle Paul said, "For me, to live is Christ, and to die is gain" (Phil. 1:21). Such should be the lives we live so that whether we know the timing of the return of Jesus Christ or not, we will not be caught off guard or be in darkness but sober and awake, with our lamps trimmed and our oil burning.

Numerous people are working so hard, saving up for retirement while they put off those desired vacation plans to travel and enjoy life, but sadly and unfortunately, many won't live to see retirement or be healthy enough to spend and benefit from all that money they've been saving. Would it not have been better to wisely enjoy life on the journey to retirement and then let it climax when you get there? It is therefore a grave and colossal mistake to neglect accepting Jesus Christ and living for Him today in the hopes of seeing enough prophetic signs in time to make that all-important and eternal decision. For too long, many have been viewing heaven just as a destination, but it's time to start seeing heaven as a journey, with Christ in us the hope of glory (Col. 1:27).

I would encourage and challenge everyone to not make the mistake of living for tomorrow while letting today go to waste. Yes, the return of Jesus Christ is a certainty, but living to see it is not guaranteed to any of us. Therefore, it is wise to live today as if there's no guarantee for tomorrow—keeping our lives pure, and living for the Lord, since there is no second chance beyond the grave. Such was the understanding of a wise man who said, "Teach us to number our days, that we may gain a heart of wisdom" (Ps. 90:12).

There is not one person, dead or alive, who will not be affected by Jesus' return. Some of us are anticipating His return, while others would like to postpone or cancel it. The scriptures tell us, however, that even the Lord looks forward to His return. Let us be ready to meet Jesus as Lord and Savior in death or in life at His return, because He is true to His word and promises. He is coming again—and according to Bible prophecy and world events, His return is near.

It's worth it to be ready...

Printed in the United States
By Bookmasters